Case Made!

10 Powerful Leadership Principles that Win Hearts, Change Minds, and Grow Impact

Tiffany Manuel, PhD

The CaseMade Press

Case Made! 10 Powerful Leadership Principles that Win Hearts, Change Minds, and Grow Impact

Larger quantities of this book may be purchased for educational, business or sales promotions by emailing Admin@TheCaseMade.com.

This book is updated frequently with additional modules, learning guides, examples, and case studies. For more information or to get regular updates, please visit www.TheCaseMade.com.

Library of Congress Cataloging-in-Publication Data has been applied for.
ISBN 978-1-7348685-1-7

For My Mom, Charline Manuel,
an accomplished author in her own right,
who inspires me every day to be better.

For my sons,
Madu and Caleb,
to whom I hope to leave a better world.

For my amazing colleagues at TheCaseMade, who
help me reimagine how justice wins everyday.

Building the public will necessary to transform the systems that shape the future of our communities, is one of the most critical challenges of our time.

Strategic CaseMaking

We live in a world of infinite possibility. We have been endowed with more than enough natural resources to build virtually whatever we put our minds to and to feed every living soul on the face of our planet. We've figured out how to cure, treat or at least, diagnose almost all human afflictions and we've proven that even in the face of a global pandemic, we can adjust our lives to fit the survival needs of our communities.

Yet when we look at national indicators of wellbeing, of hope and aspiration, we seem to be disconnected from that potential. Those indicators suggest that we are more anxious, stressed, and sanguine about our future together than we have been in decades. We're not sure that our leaders always have our best interests at heart and our trust of them (and each other) is at record low levels. We don't always see the "people who live next door" as our "neighbors" and our public policies don't always lift up our intentionality as neighbors, friends, colleagues, family, or others with whom we have common interests or shared stake.

Pundits have offered many reasons for this ironic circumstance – a world full of potential and opportunity in front of us, but a nation in deep consternation about its future, its connections, trust of each other, and its shared future.

Strategic CaseMaking is fundamentally about tapping into and reigniting that sense of potential, of infinite possibility, to leverage what we might accomplish together, and to move forward with great dispatch, all of the good uses of our collective power for each other's good.

To do that, we've got to harness people's energies toward bigger aspirations. We've got to change the energy in the rooms that we are in and connect to people's fundamental desire for good and hope for the future. And we've got to be radically inclusive – inviting everybody to be part of the future that we're building. The latter means engaging people differently, more meaningfully, and more authentically.

I've spent most of my career honing the strategies in this book, working deeply to advance issues of equity and liberation, and then studying the social science of persuasion and social movements, to maximize all that we do in the service of collective good. The good news is that there are so many great examples – both large and small, from our present and from history - to help those of us who are on the journey to justice, to make an even stronger case about the world we know is possible and to bring others along on the journey.

Let me give an example, one from the history books, that might resonate with you.

In 1961, for the first time in history, a man boarded a rocket and was launched into outer space. To the dismay of the president of the United States at the time, John F. Kennedy, that man was not an American. He was the Soviet cosmonaut, Yuri Gagarin.

President Kennedy felt strongly that losing the space race to the Soviet Union would put democracy in danger around the globe. He believed that the urgency of the moment required a bold goal to do something that had never been done before. A goal that he believed would both change the world for the better and prevent a great deal of loss. A leadership moonshot. To succeed, he needed to test his convictions with politicians and the public and get a lot of different kinds of people on his side. He needed to start building his case.

In his May 1961 address to Congress, President Kennedy made the case that space exploration was a battle for the hearts and minds of people everywhere.

He said: *"If we are to win the battle that is now going on around the world between freedom and tyranny, the dramatic achievements in space which occurred in recent weeks should have made clear to us all ... the impact of this adventure on the minds of men everywhere, who are attempting to make a determination of which road they should take."*

While Kennedy's appeal convinced Congress to give NASA the money it needed to accelerate the space program, the American people remained skeptical of the whole endeavor – and alarmed at the price tag. To achieve his ambitious space exploration goals – and beat the Soviets in the global battle for hearts and minds – Kennedy knew he needed to get the public on his side, too.

In September 1962, in front of an audience of more than 40,000 at Rice University in Houston, Kennedy delivered a speech that solidified public support for the space program for years to come. In just one of the magical moments in that speech, he said: *"We **choose** to go to the moon. We choose to go to the moon in this decade and do the other things, not because they are easy, but because they are hard, because that goal will serve to organize and measure the best of our energies and skills, because that challenge is one that we are willing to accept, one we are unwilling to postpone, and one which we intend to win, and the others, too."*

Kennedy's **"We Choose to Go to the Moon"** speech tapped deeply into the American psyche. He told a story in which Americans were the heroes of a global battle for freedom. And he convinced us that American ingenuity – with enough money and support from everyday people – we would find solutions to the technical challenges we still faced. And, on top of it all, he didn't say we'd do it "someday." He said we'd do it in less than 10 years.

We all know how that story ended, but at the time there were no guarantees. Whatever your personal convictions about President Kennedy or the space race, I think we can all agree that his was a heroic quest successfully propelled by the strategy of good casemaking. There are a number of examples throughout history of heroic quests punctuated by transformative casemaking: Dr. Martin Luther King, Jr's, "I Have a Dream" speech at the 1963 March on Washington electrified the civil rights movement.

Or then-Illinois State Senator Barak Obama's quest for unity, boldly described in his 2004 Democratic National Convention speech, in which he said:

"There is not a liberal America and a conservative America – there is the United States of America. There is not a Black America and a White America and Latino America and Asian America – there's the United States of America."

Those movement-making speeches all had something in common. Though we didn't know it at the time, President Kennedy, Dr. King, and President Obama were using the principles that a growing body of social science research tells us are necessary to rally people behind sweeping social change. I call that group of evidence-based principles **Strategic CaseMaking**. And while these movement leaders had great speech writers, there are plenty of movement makers who have moved social movement forward with principles they intuitively knew would be important – Fannie Lou Hamer's 1964 speech in Mississippi for example, or more recent speeches by movement building casemakers for climate change, racial justice, criminal justice reform, health equity, economic and housing justice – should give us all excitement about what's possible. That is, what's possible when we get our casemaking right!

The good news is that anyone can become a better casemaker with these proven principles in hand. I see good casemaking by everyday people in a lot of social movements today by people who are fighting for justice in every corner of our nation. I also know that a lot of the best casemaking goes largely unnoticed, which is one of the reasons I wrote this book. I wanted people who are making "good trouble" in the world, to have some way to know that they are doing the absolute best they can to bring new champions forward.

The bad news is that our world is getting more complex, more divisive, and more challenging, as we grow the movements that get at the root causes of our collective woes and free our nation's systems of the "isms" (racism, sexism, nationalism, ableism, and a host of other "isms"). Despite the environments that we find ourselves, finding liberatory spaces to reimagine how justice wins is critical and Strategic CaseMaking is part of that journey.

This is important - if we aren't thoughtful and strategic about how we make the case for change and about how we enroll the support of new champions, we'll lose the power and possibility that this moment is offering. This moment is about setting humankind on a more just and sustainable path and we are the frontline workers necessary to get this done - FINALLY.

That's why we need everyday heroes like you -- who are on quests for justice big and small -- to join our community of casemakers and build an active practice of reimagining how justice wins.

<u>Inside This Book</u>

In these pages, you'll find the core principles of Strategic CaseMaking, along with a series of examples, reflection questions, and resources for deploying the principles across your community, coalition, or organization. Strategic CaseMaking is a process of exploring and crafting language around your vision of the future in ways that authentically and effectively connect it to the aspirations of the people, institutions, organizations, agencies, businesses or groups you hope to mobilize to manifest that vision. It involves intentional and strategic thinking, which ultimately means that you have to put in the work and time it takes to land on it.

Learning to expertly deploy the principles outlined in this book, takes time and the space to practice. In the trainings, workshops and keynotes offered to teach Strategic CaseMaking, the goal is always to give people the time and space away from their day-to-day to-do lists, to really engage and think about what connects the work they do to the audiences they fundamentally need to advance it meaningfully.

What you won't find in this book is the perfect cookie-cutter language to drop into your next fundraising appeal or report. That answer really doesn't exist – no matter what anyone tells you. But if you work the principles in this book, those answers get a lot closer and you'll see the results in your efforts to mobilize the champions you need for real, transformative social change.

Sometimes in my keynotes, I share a picture of the Reverend, Dr. Martin Luther King, Jr. It is one of my favorites of him. He's sitting at his desk in his home office, and he is surrounded by books. On every surface - on the floor, in his hand, on the desk, on tables behind him, on his lap – literally everywhere in his office, he is surrounded with open books. He is in deep thought and I can just imagine him there, writing the *I Have a Dream* speech and trying to find just the right language to motivate a nation to get on the justice journey. Not only bringing new champions to the cause of freedom but trying to unite a deeply divided civil rights movement to work together for the bigger good. I like to think that he was able to do that because he took the time and space in that home office to study, hone his casemaking, and get strategic. From all accounts that I have read, that's exactly what he did and our nation is better because of it.

That's what this book offers as an invitation to you. It takes time and space to think strategically about how you present the justice work that you are doing and to practice so that you get better and stronger at it. Remember that for Dr. King, it took years of literally pounding the pavement with other faith leaders, activists, and everyday people to help move civil rights legislation.

Yes, I recognize that Dr. King was just one of many people, organizations, and movements working during the 1960s to uplift civil rights, that his work stood on the shoulders of thousands who came before him and with the many women warriors for justice who stood beside him but did not get the attention of public media. I recognize King and the thousands of forgotten justice workers who moved our nation.

And yet, as a student and teacher of casemaking I know that no one can deny the incredible ability of Dr. King to bring new champions – diverse, multi-racial, people across economic backgrounds and across faiths, to the service of justice. That unique skill set as an adaptive leader takes time, practice, and patience to sharpen. This book is fundamentally about that skill set.

All casemakers need this kind of patience and time to practice building the skill set embodied in adaptive leadership. So, take the time to read the chapters in this book with great reflection.

Underline what jumps out at you, practice what feels tough for you, nod vigorously when you hit casemaking skills that you are already good at and pass the wisdom of what is in these pages to your fellow justice travelers.

Remember too that more than a year passed between President Kennedy's speech to Congress about funding the space program and his speech to the American people about reaching the moon. And then it took years of reinforcement by a variety of people across the country between President Kennedy's death in 1963 and Neil Armstrong's first step on the moon in 1969.

At **TheCaseMade,** an organization that I founded, we partner with communities and organizations that have a passion for the hard work of making the world a better place for all people. Our casemakers have a commitment to equity, a desire for deep learning, a capacity for engaged listening, an openness to working differently than they have before, and the goal of bringing a more just world into our future. If that describes you and members of your organization, agency, or coalition, this book is likely to be helpful.

And, if your ultimate goal is a just world, join us.

Table of Contents

Adaptive leaders help us visit the future today and prepare us for what we'll need when we get to that future.

Facing the Future, Together, Differently

One of the things I've learned most about persuading ordinary people to become extraordinary champions of social justice, is that they are exponentially more motivated to act when they think about the future. The social science on this issue is clear – most people are much more optimistic about their lives and our ability to solve the toughest challenges in front of us, when they are positioned to think about the future. Think about it – the future hasn't happened yet, and we have the ability to mold it in any way we want.

Future pacing is just one of the many skills of adaptive leaders. Adaptive leaders know how to help people visit the future and prepare for what we'll need to get there. They know when they need to shift the energy in the room so that their stakeholders get re-energized about the journey and have a skill set that underscores how to shift people into looking toward the future.

Strategic CaseMaking is an evidence-based set of principles that helps everyday people develop the leadership skills they need to build public and political will on tough issues where consensus and coalition building are critical. It recognizes that there a set of skills, like future pacing, that everyday leaders can use to help bring new champions to solve the most important challenges of our time.

Adaptive leaders who understand the principles of Strategic CaseMaking also understand the nature of the challenges we face today. They do not see those challenges solely as a series of technical challenges that are best solved by assembling experts only. Alternatively, they understand that most of the toughest problems we face in our nation today, indeed in our world today, are adaptive problems, not technical ones.

A technical problem is one that can often be fixed with a single or momentary solution and usually requires an expert with specialized knowledge on that issue. That is, a single discovery or technological development is most often required to fix our technical problems.

For example, losing wi-fi is a technical problem. You can just restart the router or reconnect your device, and the hair-pulling chaos that ensued from being temporarily disconnected and inconvenienced, is immediately relieved and quickly forgotten. That's a technical problem.

Homelessness, the opioid epidemic, health care disparities, and the racial wealth gap are all examples of adaptive challenges our nation faces. To address them effectively, we must significantly redesign the systems that govern our lives, including education, workforce development, housing, health care, transportation, criminal justice, and many more. Those shifts are a huge undertaking. They require shifts in culture, practice, mindset, processes, and relationships between many people and institutions with differing perspectives, objectives, and goals. And they require people from all walks of life getting involved and being willing to change their attitudes, their preconceptions, their fears, their approaches and often, their behavior.

When we (as advocates of social change) work in environments that treat these kinds of larger adaptive challenges as if they are technical problems, it constrains our ability to solve the real problems at their roots (rather than just their symptoms). And worse, when we talk about these kinds of adaptive challenges like they are mere technical problems to be solved by our "experts", it mutes the productive capacity of the people in our communities. It leads many to walk away from those conversations because the remedies (and the work of implementing them) don't seem to need their opinions, viewpoints or work. In this way, treating these kinds of issues as technical problems shuts down the participatory energy of the people in our communities, making it infinitely more difficult to move even the most basic reforms forward with broad public support.

Let's take our current affordable housing crisis and the housing insecurity that it has caused for millions of Americans, for example. People often say that we can solve the affordable housing challenges in America by "building more housing." Indeed, innovative companies across America are learning how to resolve the technical challenges of building houses faster and more cheaply. Modular homes, 3-D printed homes, and tiny homes are some of those technical fixes – and some can even be purchased right on Amazon.com with free delivery! If housing insecurity were simply a technical problem, we'd have fixed it already.

But housing insecurity in America is an adaptive problem. It requires us to come together and answer big questions about who we are and what we aspire to in our country. For example, how do we overcome public beliefs that owning a home is an individual investment opportunity, and part of an American Dream outcome that is about the enrichment of individual people rather than a collective investment in a future that we all benefit from? How do we get ordinary Americans to see the value in providing housing to many of the most economically vulnerable communities, not out of a sense of charity but from the vantage point of our collective wellbeing? How will we overcome not-in-my-backyard attitudes to enable us to build affordable housing that is close to transportation and jobs, near good schools, parks, and other resources for wellbeing? And better still, how will we extend the appetite to think more broadly in this way well beyond housing – to health care, education, our environment and much more.

Our oversight in recognizing these issues as adaptive means that, these challenges persist even though we have the technical means to solve them. There are no silver bullets for adaptive challenges. They can only be solved by taking the time to redesign how governments, corporations, nonprofits, houses of worship, community-based organizations, and many other institutions do their work. And that can only happen if public and political will are aligned behind the solutions.

That's where Strategic CaseMaking comes in. This approach, based on a lifetime of community practice and social science, will help you build the support you need to help people see their stake in your success and the wisdom of the justice journey that you are on. The way you make the case for the long-term solutions that are part of your work, makes a huge difference in whether and how people show up to make the world a more just place for everyone.

So, you may be asking – how do I know if the work I'm doing needs casemaking?

Here's a rule of thumb - if the work that you are doing requires significant shifts in regulations, policies, investments, or other actions at a level of scale that can only be achieved by aligning a multitude of stakeholders, across sectors, neighborhoods, communities, organizations, and groups – you need casemaking! You have an adaptive challenge on your hands, and you'd better read this book carefully.

It is perhaps most important to say that adaptive challenges require **inclusive** systems change, almost by definition. That is, you cannot solve adaptive challenges without aligning a wide range of stakeholders and strategic partners.
And it is worth saying that most of the large, lingering crises that we face as a nation (climate change, health disparities, economic inequality, racial segregation, religious freedoms, racial equity, gun violence, and many more, etc.) could benefit from this approach.

It is also important to note that adaptive challenges require leaders who have a more nuanced skill set. Adaptive leaders thrive in environments where the task is building consensus among diverse (and sometimes opposing) stakeholders. Their challenge is building a sense of cohesion and "can do" among people unaccustomed to working together to bring about new ways of thinking and working.

Characteristics of Adaptive Leaders

 People Centered, Collaborative, and Impact Focused

 Seeks Out the Support and Alignment Across a Wide Range of Stakeholders

 Holds a Systems Orientation That Focuses on Root Causes

 Invites Public Deliberation and Collective Problem Solving

 Requires that People Shift Their Mindsets, Perspectives, Understanding, Biases, Expectations,

 Focuses on Solutions, Scale Innovation, and Manages to Our Strengths

 Is Data-Informed, Makes Evidence-Based Decisions, and Tracks Success Metrics Over Time

 Builds the Capacity of All Stakeholders to Actively Participate in Shaping the Vision

Changemakers are inherently adaptive leaders.

We understand the importance of casemaking and the intentionally strategic work that it requires.

The Urgency to Build Public Will

We are fortunate to live in a time of enormous opportunity and potential. The technological advances we've made over the last century have improved our lives beyond measure, advancing several economic, social, and health indicators in our communities.

While we may have made these important advances and though our future is bright, there remains much to be done. We don't want to take the old challenges of inequality, poverty, racial division, and social exclusion into our future. We don't want to leave a damaged planet for our kids or grandkids. We don't want a world where violence continues to be our experience.

Yet, many of the systems that govern our communities today were not designed to solve the problems we face today. They were designed for a different time and to solve different ends. Many of those systems were designed to foster racial and economic divisions and to maintain racial inequities. Today, those systems reflect deep divisions that have become calcified, even as we've fought to strip explicit forms of discrimination out of public policies. Because racial and economic divisions have been sown into the structure of our institutions, our work is even more necessary and challenging.

We must bring real focus and intentionality to the work to reimagine and redesign the systems that govern our lives. Without the intentionality to redesign them for the challenges we face today, those systems will continue to exacerbate old inequalities and create new ones – even when new policies are not crafted with discrimination in mind and do not explicitly attempt to do so. Old dividing lines of race, gender, and class are joined by new divisions along the lines of religion, political party, sexual orientation, ablism, and more.

Perhaps most important, our ability to have civil discourse about these issues and to problem-solve together is deeply challenged, requiring us to also bring an explicit lens of collaboration and consensus building to the table. Whether on the soccer field, on the nightly news, in Congressional chambers, or with our neighbors and friends – talking about the issues that shape our lives, has become more divisive and stressful than ever before. So, we must bring new skills to the table, if our work to advance a just nation is to be taken seriously.

Defining Justice
In this current environment, people doing systems change work, face stiff headwinds especially if the outcome they seek is justice. By seeking justice, I mean that we are actively identifying and

removing systemic barriers, opening access to resources and opportunities to all but especially to those who have been marginalized previously. Justice means also redressing the harms of the past and bringing a fresh perspective on how we move forward with shared fate and prosperity for all, as the outcome we seek. Working toward justice can take many forms – distributive or redistributive justice, procedural justice, etc. But no matter how we define justice, the important point is that we're always working toward some version of it.

Justice is a journey; it is not a destination. When we look across our nation and all of us, have what we need to survive and thrive, with dignity and protection for a set of unalienable human rights, living without fear of violence or harm, acknowledging the truth of our shared history – that's when we know we are getting closer to the thing called "justice".

We are far from this goal post today but there are an infinite number of paths to get us there. A multitude of policies, programs, investments, and services are on the road to a more just nation and this book is written for those travelers on this road. The goal is that we might strengthen the skill set we need to invite more people on this path and to accelerate our speed on the justice pathway.

To do both things, we need to reimagine how justice wins. One part of that winning strategy is about mobilizing more champions in support of the deeply transformational systems-change work that has to get done in the service of justice. In other words, we need more people who are in it for the long haul and who are willing to do the heavy lifting that justice work requires.

Justice, Power, and Adaptive Leadership Are Inextricably Connected Through CaseMaking
If you have been on the justice journey for any length of time, you know one thing for sure – justice, power and leadership are inextricably connected. It isn't possible to get very far on the journey to justice, without power building and changing the behavior of our leaders.

Adaptive leaders know that working together with community stakeholders to get to solutions that are in the best interests of all of us – not just *some* of us – is power building. Adaptive leaders work from an explicit acknowledgement that justice usually works against the status quo and to get there, we need countervailing power.

Countervailing power works to "counter" the policies, institutions, dominant narratives, leaders and everyday people who protect the interests of those with privileged access to justice. Adaptive leaders know that it will take all of us, working together, making compromises, seeing each other's humanity as well as respecting our diverse points of view, to get enough countervailing power that we can change the status quo and create a meaningful pathway to justice.

We have adaptive leaders in our nation today, who are indeed working to build countervailing power. But, adaptive leaders are surely outnumbered by other leaders who fail to truly understand the assignment of leadership in today's environment. Those leaders are busy building spreadsheets of data, in hopes that the focus on data will bring new champions to the policies they hope to pass. They haven't grappled with the rise of "fake news" and "alternative facts" that limit the effectiveness of a data-focused approach. They are busy crafting clever talking points and designing expert technical solutions. Those talking points on policies and solutions can certainly help, but without a focus on casemaking, they are often missing the opportunity to challenge and dismantle the sticky dominant narratives that often stand in the way of good policymaking.

I am often astounded by well-intentioned "public awareness" campaigns, for example, that are totally counterproductive, even when their goals are generally positive. Those campaigns often reinforce implicit bias and the most pernicious stereotypes. And I am especially taken aback when the strategies for revitalizing disinvested or marginalized communities, use data, maps, and other tools to reinforce old patterns of investment that re-segregate, redline and marginalize those communities – all while purporting to serve the public good.

Leadership work has never been easy, but the current political environment has made our intentional focus on the skills of casemaking to build countervailing power, even more critical. The fragmentation we see in our country today cannot be solved by leaders who are operating out of the logic that statistics, data, or even clever campaign strategies, will result in countervailing power. Too many leaders continue to be forces for division (some without even knowing it) because they have not focused on developing the casemaking skills that can bring community stakeholders into their countervailing power. And, as a result, they end up doing more harm than good - often repeating narratives that undermine our efforts to get to justice, all while touting their desire to pursue it.

We desperately need a cacophony of people, institutions, and organizations standing up on the journey to justice, we need them to understand their role as countervailing power and we need them trained in effective casemaking.

Adaptive leaders know that mobilizing people for this journey requires that they engage differently, more authentically, more compassionately, and more skillfully. Adaptive leaders know that the assignment is fundamentally about the intention and skill of inviting more people in, not shutting people out. Adaptive leaders know that justice is inextricably about power – countervailing power!

I am hoping that this describes you!

Let's Get Clear on the Challenges We Face in Building Public Will

The lack of broader public and political will to advance just solutions should concern us deeply, not just because we need broader support but also because most of us don't fully understand why we don't already have the support we need to move forward. Don't people care? Of course, people care – they care a great deal. However, the nature of the challenges our country faces, have become more complex and dynamic over the last 30 years. That complexity requires both elected leaders and everyday people to understand much more technical information than ever before and to make decisions under even more volatile conditions.

Even more sobering, we can add to the mix a widening set of issues that can constrain our casemaking and limit our success in pulling potential champions of our work forward. Those issues like the increasingly toxic culture of political partisanship and polarization in our nation, can immobilize even the best of intentions. Other issues like the cynicism and growing fatalism that many people in our nation have about what can be done to solve the most pressing problems at hand, make it even difficult to mobilize the people we need.

We also see the constant and steady diet of misinformation (sometimes, intentionally manufactured) on social media and other so-called media outlets. Add to those concerns the negativity bias of the news media alongside the powerful interests suppressing public participation and activism through voter suppression and gerrymandering. Then, it's not hard to see why people would rather stay on their couches than to join the justice journey with us.

Fewer and fewer of us have confidence that real change can happen, that our systems of governance can be made to work FOR us, and that we'll truly benefit from all the social activism we see today. Without confidence that meaningful change is possible, most people aren't likely to put themselves in a battle that doesn't seem winnable.

Constraints on Building Public Will

Dominant Narratives that Reinforce the Status Quo

Cynicism & Lack of Public Confidence in Leaders

Misinterpretation or Skepticism of Data

Misinformation, Fake News & Alternative Facts

Thin Understanding of Governance Systems

Crisis Fatigue & Fear of Carrying the Burden

Scarcity Mindset, Self-Interest, Who is the Face at the Bottom?

Fear of Change & Path Dependence

Additional Constraints: Building Political Will

Political Partisanship & Social Fragmentation

Election Cycle & Short Policy Time Horizon

Lobbyists/Wealthy Donors Have Outsized Voice

Red Tape and Bureaucracy Protect the Status Quo

Budgets Squeezed by Increasing Expectations

Out-of-Touch with Reality of Most People's Lives

Roots Causes Are Easier to Ignore

Conquer & Divide Politics Normalized

This list of constraints partially explains why so many Americans have become bystanders in their own lives. The list is long but don't let the length of the list deter you. We have to understand why building the energy and excitement for our justice journey is more than a matter of "messaging." We may have a persuasive message, as well as data and statistics that support it, but unless we understand and effectively navigate the complexity of these constraints, we aren't likely to mobilize enough support to do much good. In light of these constraints, the problems our communities face will not be solved simply by lobbying policymakers, leading influencer campaigns, creating fact sheets to "build awareness," polling to find the "persuadables," or producing the next bleeding-heart commercial whose goal it is to shame us all into action. These tactics, which often stand-in for public will building and power building, do not get at the heart of why people feel so disconnected.

As adaptive leaders, our work is to help people get up-and-over these constraints - to remember their impulse to *"charge the hill," "dump the tea," "take the state house back,"* or *"go to the moon"* in pursuit of a better future for all. We can't simply wave away these constraints as unimportant or inconsequential. We have to understand why they have come to stand in the way of justice.

Until now, there really hasn't been an effective framework for tackling these constraints holistically. Strategic CaseMaking helps to fill the void by helping adaptive leaders understand the principles for motivating people up-and-over these constraints. That is, navigating and countering a wide range of constraints that have become tough impediments to action – impediments that keep people from seeing their stake in the success of collective deliberation and action alongside others in their communities.

CaseMaking is the very foundation on which stronger public will is possible, and we need intentional and strategic efforts to rebuild that will. There is no way around this difficult work. Specifically, our task is to acknowledge what's holding back our potential champions, to listen carefully to how they express the narratives that explain these constraints, and then to develop strategies to help them overcome or navigate around them. That's all baked into Strategic CaseMaking.

That means getting all of us - not just engaged or enraged (as some movement makers try to do) but rather and more importantly, to get us inspired about the justice journey we are on together. To be inspired about the collaboration with others and the work to redesign the systems that no longer serve us.

"A genuine leader is not a searcher for consensus but a molder of consensus."

*The Reverend
Dr. Martin Luther King, Jr.*

Navigating the Traps

Having an incomplete understanding of the constraints and impediments to action (outlined in the last chapter), means we often respond to naysayers in ways that *actually worsen* our ability to engage stakeholders. And when we do that, we ultimately lose the most important battles necessary for building and broadening our support.

When we encounter opposition, our first inclination is often to "clap back" or try to counter false or misinformation with our data. When data is unavailable or context is missing, we offer up longwinded historical explanations to justify our proposed solutions. We villainize the "bad actors" to try to show why our cause is just. We use crisis framed language and big "scary" numbers about the problem, to try to scare people into urgent action. And, if all else fails, we share lots of personal stories of people's hardship and peril, hoping others will act from a sense of empathy to the needs of those who are struggling.

While these tactics can sometimes deliver short-term wins, if our goal is long-term systems change leading to justice, then they are traps. They distract the focus from casemaking that delivers on more meaningful social change - doing more harm than good.

The Don'ts:

Avoid These Responses at All Costs

- Myth versus Fact Sheets

- Negatively Framed Data or Data Solely about the Problem

- Crisis Stories and Language

- The "Clap-Back": Directly Responding to the Negative Disruptors

- History Lessons About the Perils of Systems, People or Groups

- Villainizing the People, Organizations or Groups that You Need to Change Policy and Systems

- Overly Complex Descriptions of Your Work or the Problem

- Overly Partisan Perspectives

- Hardship Stories that to Try to Elicit Empathy, Charity or Shame

We do not wish or imagine a return to the way things were.

Case Made!

46

Of course, the intentions behind each of these practices are good ones. They assume that people can be motivated to act if they understand the issues we care about as: urgent, complex, long-term, large-scale crises that are being exacerbated by bad people, making self-interested and/or bad decisions. Some or all the latter may be true of the issues on which we are working but reminding people of any of these things rarely brings forward the response we need.

What happens often is that we scare and shame people into **bystander status**. Who wants to deal with this "mess" after a long day of work!

While fear and shame are powerful motivators, if we are not careful about how we handle and navigate around those emotions for our audiences, they derail our efforts for change. Fear won't help you generate the long-term, collaborative support from the stakeholders you need to advance your solutions by itself. You'll need more than that!

And, while it is important that people understand history, have access to data, understand the urgency and the challenges of solving social issues, we must be thoughtful about HOW we leverage those strategies as our call-to-action.

When we are not strategic in our response – when we fail to make an effective and compelling case for change - our attempts to call people to action typically end in one of three ways: (1) *backfires* (unintended and counter-productive responses from stakeholders who oppose or ignore our calls to justice); *backpacks* (small or marginal policy, regulatory, and system reforms, rather than the transformative changes we need); *bedtime stories* (rejection of our call-to-action with a reference to an out-of-date belief system or perspective gained early in life). Let's take a moment to dig more deeply into these responses.

- **The Backfires.** Too often, we let our data and research about the challenges facing our communities take the place of a strong case. Not only do we overestimate the extent to which data, research, and evidence can move public support for action, we underestimate how much they can trigger resistance in people who feel disconnected from these issues more generally or who disagree with the broader set of solutions we propose. Moreover, using negatively framed or problem-focused data – especially when we are trying to advance equity issues – can further embed the implicit biases that are already at the root of so many of the social ills we are trying to solve. If we fail to anticipate the backfires, we ultimately undermine our ability to gather new champions to support the work.

- **The Backpacks.** If we fail to frame our concerns as system problems, we risk them being dismissed, undermined and under-resourced. This is in part because our instinct is to solve problems where we see them occur, mostly at the level of individuals or communities. If we don't expose the system-level challenges that are at the root of the problems we are trying to solve, the support we get amounts to consolation prizes (small victories or backpacks). While it is true that many of the problems our society faces can and should be addressed at multiple levels, we are missing the opportunity to make important system reforms more impactful.

- **The Bedtime Stories**. Our attitudes, opinions, and expectations about our lives and the ways we think about the world, were largely shaped as children. Bedtime stories not only put many of us to sleep at night, but they also helped our parents and caregivers convey how the world works, what we should value, and who the "bad guys" are. Those stories are still with us. We may be all grown up today but the basic ideas that characterized our bedtime stories are still with us, structuring how we see the world. When we, as changemakers, fail to recognize the power of those stories in shaping the attitudes of those whose support we hope to gain, we can hopelessly spin-our-wheels trying to talk people out of those engrained ideas but often fail to do so. Our task, instead, is to route people around them. We put people in the future and give them new ways to think about issues that do not trigger those old ideas. Putting people in the future is very important (as we will discuss later in this book) because, the future is something we can create together, not a story that has already been written. Carefully rooting people in our shared history but helping them navigate to the future is one of the most important techniques of casemaking. For that reason, we'll return to this idea.

Making the case by starting with any of the traps outlined above, is a sure-fire way to get hit with backfires, backpacks, and bedtime stories!

Strategic CaseMaking (as outlined in this book) helps us engage people effectively, to understand the constraints and navigate around them so that we avoid triggering backfires, backpacks, and bedtime stories. On any issue for which we are working, we need to know:

- *Where are the backfires?*
- *What are the backpacks that people are willing to offer in lieu of true system change?*
- *What are the bedtime stories that people tell themselves about the problem, that limit how they respond to the case we are making?*

Once you've thought carefully about those, you'll have the first of the many insights needed to craft a compelling case.

Reflection Question

DON'T RAISE YOUR VOICE, IMPROVE YOUR ARGUMENT.

Desmond Tutu

South African Social Rights Activist and Anglican cleric who in
1984 received the Nobel Prize for Peace for his role in the
opposition to apartheid in South Africa.

What is Strategic CaseMaking™?

Strategic CaseMaking is an evidence-based set of principles that helps everyday people develop the leadership skills they need to build public and political will on tough issues where consensus and coalition building are critical. It recognizes that there a set of skills that everyday leaders can use to help bring new champions to solve the most important challenges of our time.

At the most basic level, casemaking is the work to move the impediments to action out of the way so that our champions (new and existing), can hear our calls-to-action.

If you've been on the road to justice for any length of time, it's likely that you already have some casemaking skills in your toolbelt. But unless you've done some intentional work around those skills, it's also likely that they could use some sharpening, honing and improvements to maximize the effectiveness of your call to action.

Most of us have learned how to present logical arguments with our data and evidence. It's hard to advance any cause without some ability to make an argument about what solutions would help. Some of us have even become fairly good storytellers and have the ability to explain the challenges our communities face and why change is necessary. Yet our explanations, stories and data can miss the mark when we do not recognize and anticipate how they will be received by our stakeholders – most of whom already have beliefs, opinions, and thoughts about how the world works. And if our goal is to advance our justice seeking as far as we can, then we need every cylinder firing as much and as hard as we can get them moving.

Strategic CaseMaking represents a way to learn the kind of adaptive leadership skills that can help you win more champions, broaden your support, and diversify the stakeholders coming to your aid. And if the aspiration is to maximize the ground we can cover, isn't that worth the investment of time, patience, and energy?

Stra·te·gic Case·Ma·king
[*struh-tee-jik* **keys**-*mey-king*]

1: *(noun)* a set of leadership principles that helps everyday people change the narrative, build public will, and achieve systems change. This is especially important where justice, equity, and inclusion are critical drivers and outcomes of the work. This approach actively anticipates stakeholders' impediments to action and gives leaders the tools to respond strategically.

2: *(verb)* mobilizing support from community stakeholders to pursue justice and equity-focused solutions - especially on issues where consensus and coalition building are critical.

That's where Strategic CaseMaking comes in. It's about learning the skills, principles and techniques that allow you to invite a more thoughtful public discourse; a public discourse that helps people see their stake in your success and builds a broader sense of trust, belonging, and agency to the issues you are trying to solve.

Strategic CaseMaking is not communications; it is leadership skill building. Because casemaking can be easily confused with communications or narrative change efforts, it is important to make the distinctions clear. CaseMaking is the foundational work that must happen before an effective communications strategy can be crafted. It focuses on helping adaptive leaders better assess the impediments to action that often keep people from leaning forward on issues that need their participation.

Strategic CaseMaking is not narrative change; strong narratives can help or hurt the case that we are making but shifting or changing the narratives doesn't make your case. As we are making a case for particular solutions, we have to be mindful that popular or dominant narratives can help or hurt the case that we are making. If those narratives help our case, our goal is to leverage those narratives as part of our casemaking.

Too often on issues of equity and justice however, the dominant narratives work against us – pitting harmful mental models or ways of thinking against us. In the latter case we either have to navigate around those dominant narratives or reframe the conversation entirely, and that affects the larger story we are telling about our solutions.

So, narrative change (by itself) is not enough to make your case. A good narrative can support your case, but it cannot make your case. Think of it in this way, a good supportive narrative is like soil that is well fertilized. It allows you to plant any number of flowers, or vegetables or trees in it and have them grow. But soil, in and of itself, won't grow those things. Instead, think of narrative change efforts as opportunities to get the soil ready for the plants you are trying to grow (i.e. the case you are trying to make).

Strategic CaseMaking is not about preaching to the converted; it is about aligning and mobilizing diverse groups of institutions, community residents, agencies, organizations, corporations, houses of worship, community and social groups who are working toward better outcomes for all of us. CaseMaking is really oriented toward adaptive leaders who understand that power building is best accomplished by bringing diverse groups together to solve common ends. Our task is to bring people together in ways that give us countervailing power.

Finally, Strategic CaseMaking is not meant to convince everybody of your cause (convincing EVERYBODY is an unrealistic goal). Not everybody can be won over through casemaking. That's not a flaw of casemaking but rather an acknowledgement that we won't win over everybody. And, while we may not win everybody, we HAVE TO win over some of the people, institutions or stakeholders who may today oppose our work or perspective. This gives us a fighting chance to engage those bystanders thoughtfully.

Distinguishing Our Terms

Strategic Communications: Supports leaders in raising awareness around key social issues. Conveys a perspective and tries to convince others to take up that perspective. Key focus on delivering a message in different ways, like social media, press releases, advocacy events, etc.

Narratives: Repeated stories that remind us who we are, how we got here, and what needs to be done to shape the future we envision. When we align the narratives around our issues, we set up a foundation on which the work to bring about systems change, equity, diversity and justice are operationalized.

Dominant Narratives: Unquestioned "truths" that have been normalized by society and feel like common sense. They are amplified in the policies, organizations, and institutions that govern us, and are reinforced by social norms that ensure their longevity. Because they reflect the status quo, they typically amplify individualism, sexism, racism, ablism, nationalism, homophobia and other oppressive power dynamics.

Narrative Change: Disrupting or unseating the dominant narratives that normalize inequity and uphold oppression, to make way for the dominance of new narratives that help us dismantle social inequities and imagine a different future.

Strategic CaseMaking: The strategic deployment of casemaking skills – the leadership skills needed to operationalize narrative change and build public will around deeply transformational system change work. This is especially important where justice, equity, diversity, and inclusion are critical drivers and outcomes of the work. This approach actively anticipates the impediments to action and gives leaders the tools to respond strategically.

Get Your Ground Game Ready

CaseMaking principles and skills are meant to help you on your journey for a more just and equitable world – but they are not the journey itself. For your casemaking to succeed, you have to have some things figured out first: *who you are, what you're seeking, how you're going to get there, and some idea of who you need to come along with you.*

Having this foundational work figured out is important because, through your casemaking, you are asking people to commit their time and energy to your quest. You're asking them to leave the comfort of what they already know and take risks with you – risks to their reputation and of losing out on opportunities to make an impact elsewhere.

CaseMaking to Different Types of Stakeholders
No matter what issues or systems redesign you are trying to advance, you face the challenge of needing to make your case to different stakeholders at different levels of power. Those stakeholders are likely to have different roles, goals, ways of working and communicating, as well as different appetites for information, data, and storytelling norms.

It's important to understand these differences as you craft your case. Having to advance your case with stakeholders at these different levels of power – and sometimes all at once – can present its own set of challenges, so let's get clear on the fundamentals.

At the outset, it is helpful to differentiate at least three types of stakeholders.

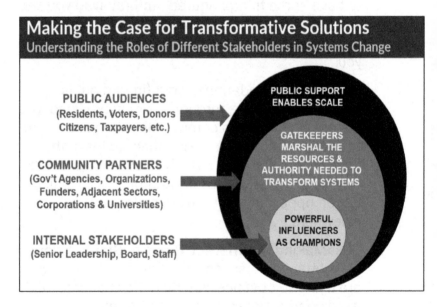

Making the Case for Transformative Solutions
Understanding the Roles of Different Stakeholders in Systems Change

PUBLIC AUDIENCES
(Residents, Voters, Donors
Citizens, Taxpayers, etc.)

COMMUNITY PARTNERS
(Gov't Agencies, Organizations,
Funders, Adjacent Sectors,
Corporations & Universities)

INTERNAL STAKEHOLDERS
(Senior Leadership, Board, Staff)

PUBLIC SUPPORT
ENABLES SCALE

GATEKEEPERS
MARSHAL THE
RESOURCES &
AUTHORITY NEEDED TO
TRANSFORM SYSTEMS

POWERFUL
INFLUENCERS
AS CHAMPIONS

1. First, those stakeholders closest to your work, coalition or organization should be your first priority. This could be community residents around you or your internal organizational stakeholders like your Board of Trustees, senior leadership team, or organizational staff, and their support should always be solidified first. As the saying goes, put your life mask on first and then work to preserve that of others around you!

②. Second, your community partners in government agencies, corporations, nonprofits, universities, and other institutions in your eco-system are important because they often operate as gatekeepers of important resources needed to advance the work. Gaining their support often enables you to have the resources and broader network of institutional champions necessary to start or engage the work in earnest.

③. Third but certainly no less important, is the broader public (and that often includes broader residents across the region, voters, donors, taxpayers, etc.) whose support can give us the opportunity to scale the solutions we know would work. It is the support from the broader public that is often the most elusive and difficult for casemakers because there are so many different groups of people who need to be won over at this level.

Recognizing Stakeholder Impediments to Action
Opinion polling on social issues can be an important source of information about how people think about issues. I have seen polls used thoughtfully in many circumstances to gauge public reaction to tough issues on many topics.

However, many social changemakers have learned the hard way that people's general opinions about issues does not easily translate into support or action. Take for example opinion polling on issues like health care, gun safety laws, and affordable housing. Polling data in most parts of the country generally favor more investments in solutions to these issues. Yet when people are asked if they would be willing to advocate or do something to help bring the solutions they favor to life, their support can quickly evaporate. That means, those opinions are largely theoretical unless we can find ways to make that support real.

When our stakeholders fail to take up arms with us, especially when our polling tells us that they agree with our goals, we are often perplexed. Moving people from their grandiose opinions about how the world _should_ work, to their _active participation_ in working toward that just world, is the skill set we sharpen with casemaking.

We need to be keen on understanding the impediments that keep people from acting on their beliefs. The discernment that we need comes from listening carefully to our stakeholders so that we get to address the specific impediments to action at play in our relationships with them.

For example, a common impediment on many issues that require collective action, is the lack of a sense of shared stake or shared fate among the people we need to support our efforts. If our stakeholders do not feel as though they have a stake in our success or in solving the issue at the heart of our efforts, our solutions (however well crafted) may not get the support they may well deserve. We see this for example, in Not-In-My-Backyard (NIMBY) arguments to affordable housing.

If your challenge is to build support for more affordable housing and the stakeholders that you need support from are mostly homeowners (who already have stable and affordable housing), they may not come out to support affordable housing because they don't see their stake in solving that issue in their own lives. So to be clear - their opinions may be supportive of affordable housing as a worthy goal for the larger society but their willingness to act on it in their neighborhoods may be minuscule because they don't see this issue as something that would positively and deeply affect them.

If your response is to try to overcome these NIMBY attitudes by extolling the general wisdom of affordable housing policies or reminding them of how many people across the region or in our society, are struggling to find affordable housing, it is unlikely that you'll have much success. Your appeal will literally get lost in the emotion of separate fate.

In this case, the impediment to action is feeling separate fate, not the NIMBY attitude. So, the case you must build will need to establish a sense of shared stake/fate to help those homeowners feel connected on this issue. You'll need to remind them of what they have at stake on this issue and what shared aspiration they have in common with the people struggling to afford affordable housing in the community.

Once you can remove the impediment of separate fates (and the energy of having people feel so separate), your stakeholders can actually hear the wisdom of your call to action. So, the ability to discern that the primary issue is lack of shared fate rather than lack of interest or empathy related to affordable housing, allows us to address the real concern. When we do, we stand a much better chance of elevating our call-to-action.

Extreme political polarization is another example of an impediment to action that can challenge our ability to mobilize stakeholders. When people are as polarized and distrustful as they are in the current environment, it often means that our cause may not get the hearing it deserves because our stakeholders assume it to be aligned with one political party or another.

Once our potential champions think they know something about our political affiliation for example, they may distance themselves or reject our call-to-action even before hearing about our work. And most of all, it becomes harder to mobilize them to action when they "take sides" without actually hearing us out.

Strategic CaseMaking helps you build a strategy for navigating around political polarization. We overcome that impediment to action, not by extolling the virtues of the solutions we propose nor by trying to appeal to the fiction of some ideological unity, but rather, by framing the conversation much higher and appealing to the bigger aspirations that we all have for our lives. Be clear – the strategy here is not just a communications approach for our stakeholders, it is an adaptive leadership skill – discerning the impediments of our stakeholders and then, deploying one of the strategic principles to overcome it.

Attentively listening to stakeholders and then strategically navigating around the impediments to their action is how you connect people's ambitions, hopes, dreams to the issues in your case. The more they see **YOUR** issues as **THEIR** issues, the more effective our call-to-action will be. That's what I mean by helping people feel more "proximate" or connected to our proposed solutions.

Getting People on Your Bridge of Understanding
Imagine that you are standing on one side of a
bridge – what I call the **bridge of understanding** --
and you are planning to make your case to people
on the other side of the bridge, encouraging them
to cross over. You are asking them to act – to
move out of their inertia or bystander status and
that requires you to first think about what entices
them to take the trek across that bridge to you.

Before they step foot on your bridge, those folks
are going to size up its foundation – Is it well-
built? Will it hold all our weight? Will it get us
where we want to go and to safer ground?

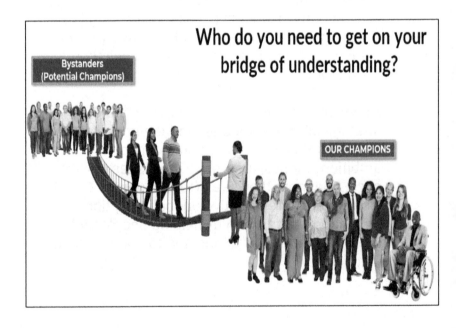

The remainder of this part of the book will help you think through whether the foundation of your bridge is strong enough to entice new champions to join you on it.

Who Are You?

For people to trust you enough to get on your bridge, they must understand and identify with who you are as a company, foundation, agency, non-profit, coalition, or movement. This starts with a clear understanding of your mission, vision and values, and the reputation you have in the spaces that you occupy.

If you don't yet have a clear identity, you'll want to spend some time developing that first – perhaps with the help of professionals through a formal branding process. That identity should be diffused throughout your organization, so that wherever people go to seek information about you – including the opinions of your own staff -- they will come away with the same authentic sense of who you are.

As part of that initial branding work, you'll want to take stock of whether you are living into the values that you say you hold. For example, it will be difficult for you to build a case for social justice or equitable systems change outside your organization, if you haven't at least begun to address inequities inside your organization through a formalized diversity, equity, and inclusion strategy that has clear and transparent benchmarks for success. It will also be hard to get a broader coalition of partners to trust your programmatic or advocacy work if your organization doesn't meaningfully include, listen to, and follow the people you serve, along with a diversity of perspectives in the community.

We, as changemakers, have a lot to learn from the world of marketing when it comes to building identity and trust. Consumers reserve their fiercest loyalty for the brands – like Apple, Nike, or Jeep – that take the time to build and nurture an authentic and consistent identity based on a set of clearly articulated values that they live into every day. If you aren't an Apple customer, you likely know many people who feel so strongly about the company that they will take time out of their day to try and convince you to switch to an iPhone or a MacBook.

Our opportunity is to build that fierce loyalty in the work to advance justice – indeed, that is core to how long-lasting successful movements are made. While we shouldn't underestimate how much time and attention this foundational, identity-building work takes, the effort will be worth it.

What Are You Seeking?

For people to join your journey, it also helps if they have a clear sense of your final destination – the bigger-picture adaptive challenge that you are trying to solve. Framing this clearly helps all kinds of people – not just your closest stakeholders – see their stake in your work, and it gives them a better sense of what they will lose if they don't join you.

Describing that destination well is often difficult for leaders who are focused more narrowly on advancing specific policies, programs or services that need their attention in the short term. One way to think bigger is to put yourself into the future. Envision a fork in the road ahead of you leading to two different tomorrows.

At the end of one road is a tomorrow where we took little or no action to solve the challenges facing us now. Where we ignored our problems and brought old inequities and divisiveness forward so that they got exponentially worse. In that tomorrow, our cities, our communities, our planet, and our people, are left barren.

The second road leads to a tomorrow where we have taken decisive action now on our biggest challenges. We have addressed current injustices, redressed past and current harms, and created a more equitable and inclusive future – one that offers up the possibility of an evergreen planet and people who are thriving.

That's the **adaptive challenge** in front of us. Either we rise to the occasion and plan today for the needs of our communities or we choose to be divided, unprepared, and at risk of the uncertainty of any future shocks. Your task is to help people to fully understand the starkness of those choices, and to position your work as contributing to that story of a better tomorrow.

To get started, ask yourself, how will your issue, policy, program, etc., help all of us to be prepared for the world that is coming in the next 20, 50, or 100 years? Why do we need to address this issue now to have a bright future, given the climate, economic, demographic, and technological shifts on the horizon? Your answers to those questions will help you tell a bigger story about your approach and the value of your solution.

Framing the Adaptive Challenge:
The Two Tomorrows

Example: School Redistricting Policy
Imagine you are a school district taking up the need for redistricting to rebalance the student population and to address equity issues across the community.

This issue is a common source of tension among community members that usually devolves into a public fight about the specifics of the redistricting policy itself. But the underlying adaptive challenge is about better serving the needs of all students and doing so in an equitable fashion so that they are fully prepared to address the challenges of the future. If we choose to fight the policy issue on its merits alone, we have little chance of bringing our stakeholders and strategic partners to the table to resolve the issue thoughtfully. So, what if we said this instead?

> **To be prepared for the economy that is coming** – *one that increasingly values a diversity of experiences, skill sets, and cultural fluency – we must give all our children rich opportunities to learn from and grow with each other, supported by teachers with the resources they need to help all our children thrive.*

In framing our adaptive challenge, we also need to be clear about the consequences for ALL of us if we don't set our kids up for success.

If we fail to solve this challenge, *we will not have the kind of skilled workforce or citizenry that we need to remain competitive in a more globalized economy. And we will take our history of social, economic, and racial inequity and injustice into the future, further sapping the energy and vitality from our community, at a time when we need them most.*

This matters for everybody because *we need all-hands-on-deck to prepare for the economy that is coming. We must drive policies that help us grow the capacity of the young people in whose care we will place the institutions that we have created in this community.*

Example: Community Health Programs

Imagine you are a community health program that is chronically under-resourced, and you spend a great deal of your time trying to convince funders to give you more money to keep your programs afloat. Direct appeals to your key stakeholders might work to fill funding gaps, but they don't give you the broad support you need to address the challenges facing us in the future related to new public health threats and a graying population. So, what if we said this instead?

To be prepared for future public health threats and to meet the needs of our aging neighbors and ourselves, *we must make sure our community has the health resources it needs to take care of all of us when we need it.*

If we fail to solve this challenge, *we simply will not have the medical care we need to keep our community healthy. And we'll take a history of social, economic and racial inequity and injustice into the future, where it will continue to literally drain the wellbeing out of our people.*

This matters for everybody in this region because *we need all-hands-on-deck to prepare for the new public health threats that are coming, so that we don't lose the productive capacity of a great number of people who could be contributing to our future.*

The benefit of taking the time to frame the adaptive challenge in this way is that we get super clear on the problem we're solving, why it matters to *everyone*, and what we lose if we don't solve it - before we try to make that case to anybody else.

It also helps set up the forward-thinking, productive mindset needed to craft a credible case for support and to motivate the people you need to hear and heed your call-to-action.

How Are We Going to Get There?

CaseMaking is, in relatively equal parts, an appeal to people's hearts and minds. Once they understand who you are and where you are headed, they need to have some confidence that your proposed solution will work and that you have a way to measure your success.

This is where your theory of change kicks in, backed by a results framework that will allow you to be honest and transparent about where you are succeeding and where adjustments need to be made.

There are plenty of good resources online to help you develop a solid theory of change, so I won't duplicate that here. Here are some additional questions you might ask yourself as you are doing that work:

- *What data and evidence has guided our solution or approach?*

- *How have people with lived experience been involved in designing, informing, and leading our solution?*

- *What was the result of an equity analysis on our solution or approach? How do we know that it is anti-racist and decolonized by design?*

- *How will our solution change inequitable and marginalizing systems and program models that impact people's lives?*

Your theory of change is another place where you may need to spend significant time before you are ready to take your case to the public. If you don't pressure test your own assumptions about the solutions you are offering, rest assured the public will do it for you!

Who Needs to Come Along With You?

Once the foundation of your bridge of understanding feels solid, it's time to start thinking through who you want on it, and in what order. Start with a blue-sky wish list of the people and partners in your community who can build momentum for your cause. That could include:

- *People with lived expertise and people from historically marginalized communities*
- *Politicians or partners from state or local government*
- *Organizers*
- *Cultural influencers*
- *Faith leaders*
- *Foundation leaders*
- *Unions (Law Enforcement, Teachers, Service Workers)*
- *Anchor Institutions (Hospitals and health systems, Houses of Worship, Universities)*
- *Community based organizations*
- *Social justice organizations*
- *Citizens groups (League of Women Voters, Rotary Clubs, HOAs)*

- *Large scale developers*
- *Small business associations*
- *Landlord or tenant associations*
- *Housing Finance Agencies*
- *Social service providers*
- *Child welfare groups*
- *Workforce Investment Boards*
- *Climate change groups*
- *Student groups*
- *Other grassroots organizations and publicly funded programs*

Once you have a comprehensive list, it's time to get strategic about who you are going to start making your case to first, second, third, and so on. These questions might help:

- *Who do we have some connection to already?*
- *Who will be the easy early adopters of our cause?*
- *Who will lend us credibility?*
- *Who has a big voice or influence?*
- *Who has strong organizing skills?*
- *Who will challenge our perspectives in helpful ways?*
- *Who is skilled at bringing others along?*
- *What identities, expertise, and experiences should be represented early on?*
- *Who will be skilled at helping us identify gaps in our early thinking?*

Phew! I know I've asked you to do a lot of work as you develop your ground game, but I promise it will pay off as we start in the next section to use Strategic CaseMaking to build the case for a future where everyone thrives.

The complex adaptive
challenges our nation faces can
only be solved when we work to
align a great number of people,
institutions, agencies,
organizations, houses of
worship, and corporate partners.

All of whom have different
attitudes, beliefs, perspectives,
biases, and interests.

We either rise to the occasion to
create a world that works for all
and that is evergreen, or we
become bystanders to our own
failure.

That's why it's tough!
That's the work!

Put the Big Rocks In First

Business consultants often spout the adage – *put the big rocks in first*. They usually say this to try to get their clients to prioritize and focus chiefly on the things that matter most. Well in this case, what is true for business consultants, is also a useful adage for those of us making the case for change. Before you craft or start to deliver your case, take the time to define the big rocks in terms of the relationships that you have with your stakeholders.

No matter who the stakeholders or strategic partners are, put the big rocks of your relationship in first.

At bare minimum, that means making sure that your stakeholders and potential champions:

- **trust** you and the validity of the case you are making

- feel that they **belong** to the group of people for which you are advocating or trying to help (belonging is powerful) and feel a sense of agency (or empowerment) to act

- perceive that they have a **stake** in your success or will benefit from it

- know that you have listened to them and **understand their experiences**

- **understand what role they play** in your success

- believe that there is added power in **working with you** (collective efficacy) and your solution has the potential to work.

These big rocks of your relationship are the building blocks on which your case will be built and part of the calculus your stakeholders will use to evaluate whether they can join you on your bridge. The most important of these rocks are trust, belonging and stake. If you miss the opportunity to position these big rocks first, it will greatly diminish your ability to make your case. And ultimately, it is unlikely that you will be able to get the support you need from your stakeholders and gain the support of new champions of your work.

People often assume away these big rocks, but it is worth the time and energy to make sure that you have the trust of the people you are talking to. If you haven't already established a working relationship with the people you are talking to – prioritize this work first. Spend time with people, engage in active listening, take note of how they talk about their pain points and aspirations. Try to see the world from their perspective and imagine what would inspire you if you were in their shoes. Do not underestimate how much time this foundational work takes.

Trust takes time to build and there are few accelerators to advance you without putting in the work here. Putting the big rocks in first means establishing the connections and relationships that enable a strong case to be made and that open people up to the ideas you want to put on the table.

"Move at the speed of trust."

Adrienne Maree Brown,
Emergent Strategy

Strategic CaseMaking™: The Social Science Behind the Approach

Finally, the super good news! There is an art and a science to making the case for change. The case that we build must work to navigate around the impediments to action that our stakeholders feel and pull people onto our bridge of understanding, closer to the solutions that matter most. That case must center equity, seek justice, and do so in a way that is radically inclusive. By radical inclusion, I mean our case must include everyone at the table – even the people, organizations, and stakeholders who we'd like to think of as villains to the story of justice. And our work must seek to get the groundswell of support we need by making our systems more visible and their redesign, the outcome of our collective work.

To do this work, we can draw from the growing body of social science and emergent strategies from community development practitioners that help us to inform and strengthen how we make the case for systems change. Strategic CaseMaking™ is a synthesis of the most powerful of those strategies. The approach outlined here is empirically based, time-tested and practical. This framework is interdisciplinary – drawing extensively from across the social sciences.

Strategic CaseMaking™

POWERFUL STORYTELLING

FRAMING & MESSAGING

VALUE PROPOSITION

SOCIAL MOVEMENTS

POLITCAL ECONOMY

It would take an additional book to review all the social science research on whose shoulders Strategic CaseMaking™ stands.

Instead, this volume is dedicated to the "how-to" of the approach. So, for now, let's suffice to say that the most foundational part of the evidence-base comes from the science behind powerful and compelling storytelling. We know that when people hear new information in the form of stories, they listen differently. They digest that information more effectively and our stories help us to convey ideas that deeply engage people's emotions, empathy and inclination for action.

We are,
as a species,
addicted to story.

Even when the body
goes to sleep, the
mind stays up all
night telling itself
stories.

Jonathan Gottschall
The Storytelling Animal:
How Stories Make Us Human

Powerful storytelling can advance our cause far beyond any data point or press release. But to be effective at helping people see the benefit of equity, inclusion and system change, our stories must be told strategically. And this is where the full spectrum of social science becomes helpful on our journey to justice.

We must become practiced at telling stories that not only inform people about the adaptive challenges we face, but that inspire them to action. In this way, this book is a storytelling guide. The following casemaking principles, when woven together, help us improve our storytelling for systems change.

If our goal is more than telling an interesting story and to mobilize people to act, our stories have to be supercharged. That means, we'll need to be better able to tell stories that help people see our solutions as deeply connected to their own aspirations and interests.

Here are just a few of the stories we need to see in order to mobilize broader public support.

We need:

- **stories that** allow us to see our collective stake and responsibility for the success of solutions on the table.

- **stories that** help us to clearly assess the advantages of urgent and thoughtful action versus the consequences of inaction.
- **stories that** help us remain accountable for the promises we make to each other and those that help us use our data to understand why our investments in each other matter.
- **stories that** remind us of our past triumphs and the times we acted in unison to achieve lofty goals.
- **stories that** make us believe that another, more equitable world is possible and that make each of us feel like our collective contributions are the ones that matter most.
- **stories that** remind us that "government" should be a collection of people trying to organize the world for the better, if only we would lift our voices to ensure it.
- **stories that** help us to be honest about the harm and trauma caused to so many people because our institutions have ground them down. Those stories should feature our intentional efforts to redress those wrongs.

We return to these storytelling archetypes as we describe the ten core principles of casemaking.

10 Core Principles of Strategic CaseMaking™

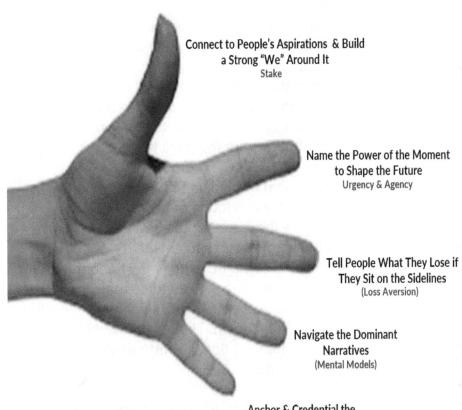

Connect to People's Aspirations & Build
a Strong "We" Around It
Stake

Name the Power of the Moment
to Shape the Future
Urgency & Agency

Tell People What They Lose if
They Sit on the Sidelines
(Loss Aversion)

Navigate the Dominant
Narratives
(Mental Models)

Anchor & Credential the
Solutions, Not Problems
(Awareness & Agency)

These core principles are evidence-based ways to make a powerful and compelling case. To start reaping the benefits of a Strategic CaseMaking™ approach, use the principles we outline here. You don't have to master all of them at once but start by connecting to people's aspirations and keep working from there.

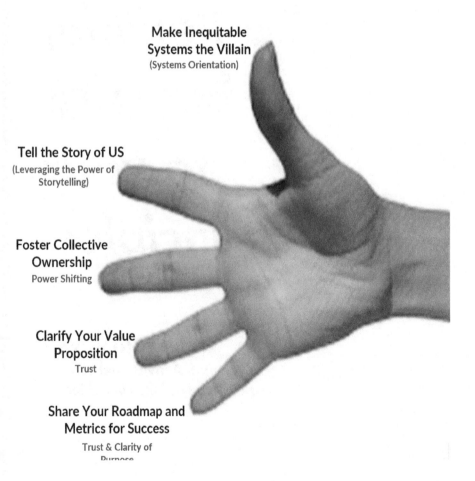

Make Inequitable Systems the Villain
(Systems Orientation)

Tell the Story of US
(Leveraging the Power of Storytelling)

Foster Collective Ownership
Power Shifting

Clarify Your Value Proposition
Trust

Share Your Roadmap and Metrics for Success
Trust & Clarity of Purpose

Be flexible, but stick to your principles.

Eleanor Roosevelt
Diplomat, Activist, and Longest
Serving First Lady of the United States

Deploying the Principles

Now that you are clear about the justice-oriented quest you are on and have done the groundwork to map the path to getting there, it's time to start digging into the principles you'll need. The ten principles that follow make up a leadership skillset that will take time and practice to perfect. They require that you have an open mind, the willingness to listen deeply to all kinds of people in your community, and the courage to do things differently – both individually and as a leader in your organization and coalition. They will require you to be both brave and humble – the marks of a true adaptive leader.

The principles are offered roughly in the order in which they should be deployed in your conversations, presentations, writings, and virtual interactions. So, Principle #1 – *Connect Your Work to People's Aspirations* – is how you should start every conversation. Then you'll want to *Name the Power of the Moment to Affect the Future*. And so on. You don't have to perfect one before moving on to the next.

Instead, think of the principles as scaffolding to build on as you engage your stakeholders. Make the principles your own - giving them the benefit of the time, patience and practice that your justice journey deserves.

For each principle we provide the following tools.

What's the Principle?
Each principle is described so that you understand what the principle is, the context for it, why it matters, how it works, and how to deploy it in your materials to make the case.

Reflection Questions
After the description of each principle, reflection questions are offered so that you can start to ask the questions that help you to strengthen how you are making the case. Use these questions to lead conversations with your team, allies, board, and other champions of

Tickets to Success
This section provides your "ticket" to better practice gleaned from real world experience across a variety of issue areas. Use these quick nuggets to get stronger in your casemaking even faster.

Pro-Tips
Use this real-world example to see how this principle has been deployed. Take notes and see if you might tailor the example to fit your casemaking.

Sample Success Metrics

Casemaking can take multiple tries to bring new strategic partners along. How do you know when you've effectively deployed a principle in your case? You'll know because you can benchmark your performance with a few sample metrics that can be useful bellwethers along the way, to help you know if we're on the right track and to mark your progress along the way.

Examples and Sample Language

We share specific language examples from real campaigns, proposals, pitch decks, and other materials that we've worked on over the years. We've changed the names and some of the information in the examples (since some of the materials are proprietary or confidential). But the goal here is to show how the principles can be deployed effectively across from different issue areas, sectors, institutional contexts, and messengers. Again, this is not "plug and play" language but rather, examples provided so that you can get a sense of what the principle looks like in a real context. More real-world examples of each principal can be found on our website (**www.TheCaseMade.com**).

"There is no power for change greater than a community discovering what it cares about."

Margaret J. Wheatley

Principle #1: Connect Your Work to People's Aspirations (Their WHY) and Build a Strong "WE" Around It

Making an effective case means speaking first to the aspirations and hopes of the people to whom we are talking. We call this their WHY – the thing that most motivates them, inspires them, and speaks to their aspirations for their own lives. When we lift up and reflect back what people want for their lives, work or community, they are more willing to hear us, even when the conversations we need to have with them are tough or require some sacrifice on their part.

This means that the success of the case we are making depends in part on our understanding the values that motivate the folks we are talking to (their WHY) and our ability to articulate how those values are shared (our WE). When we open the conversation by connecting those two (WE and WHY), we lay the foundation for our casemaking and open a story that grabs people's attention. People are much more likely to listen to our point of view when they believe we share the same values and the same animating concerns (a common WHY).

Establishing the WE and WHY first, provides your stakeholders with a sense of belonging and opens the opportunity for collective problem-solving. When we fail to establish a strong sense of WE and WHY as the lead to the case that we are making, we don't have a strong foundation for engaging their support. So, take the time to listen to and incorporate the aspirations of the people you are making your case to, as a first step toward a sense of shared stake in the issues you raise.

Reflection Questions

- Have I identified shared values that speak to the aspirations of the stakeholders hearing my case?
- Have I opened the conversation by relating those shared values (WHY) to the issues and solutions that I am proposing?
- Have I established a sense of WE (a positive collective identity) that can help position my stakeholders with enough stake and standing to problem-solve together?

Your Ticket to Implementing This Principle

There are many ways to get the information you need to advance this principle in your work. Skilled negotiators often use the practice of *mirroring*. So, instead of going off to create your own language at the top of

---

your case, listen to your stakeholders and mirror the positive language, images, visuals, identities, and behaviors that you derive from them.

Mirror them back to your stakeholders and then in an appreciative way, connect them to the work that you are doing. In this way, you are helping your stakeholders to connect their WHY, to your WHY, using what most inspires and speaks directly to them! When you do that, you'll find the shared connection that allows you both to speak in terms of "WE", which is always the basis of a strong case!

Sample Success Measures

- **KPI:** We are consistently starting our messaging by articulating our WE and WHY.
- **Outcome:** We start to hear our stakeholders using/reinforcing our We and Why.
- **Impact:** We no longer have to convince our stakeholders about why we should act because they take this as a given – prioritizing our concerns.

ASSET-BASED FRAMING
AND APPRECIATIVE INQUIRY

Although it may not seem like it at first, there's a lot going on in this first principle which advises us to seek out a WE and a Why first. There are many skills to get there – mirroring can help (*a skill that we discussed previously in Your Ticket to Implementing This Principle*). Two other skill sets to use here are asset-based framing and appreciative inquiry.

Asset-Based Framing

At the most basic level, asset-based framing and appreciative Inquiry are twin processes. Asset-based framing in the context of casemaking is about engaging people and their communities through their aspirations and contributions before any conversation about their problems, challenges, lack or limitations, take place. Asset-based framing assumes that communities had value <u>before</u> the nonprofit showed up, or that kids have value even <u>before</u> and <u>after</u> they take standardized tests, no matter their scores. It means refusing to label people as "at-risk" or characterizing them as "homeless", discussing the problems they face, and then asking others to join in a conversation that sees them as "other" or deficit.

Unfortunately, most of us in the social justice space start there – in deficits, problems, lack and limitations. Too many of us start our casemaking with negative framing of the very people and places that we are trying to help. We do this because we want people to focus on the things that need to get fixed.

But this kind of framing dooms the work from the very beginning - defining the conversation by all of the things that are going wrong and labeling people by their problems, rather than the attributes of which they are proudest. The effect is that our opening salvo demoralizes the very people that we are working so hard to mobilize - ultimately making it harder to achieve the task.

When we open the conversation with asset-based framing instead, we change the energy in the conversation and enable people to operate from a position of strength rather than their faults. Starting by defining ourselves as innovators, pioneers, good neighbors, etc., and giving examples of when we have exhibited those behaviors, sets the tone for the conversation we hope to have with them.

Appreciative Inquiry

To deepen this sense of strength, we ask follow-up questions from a place of appreciative inquiry. Appreciative inquiry is the art of asking unconditional, positive questions to strengthen people's capacity to anticipate and look forward to solving hard challenges – which is ultimately what we want them to do.

When we ask questions that appreciate who people already are (asset-based framing) and then ask questions from the vantage point of appreciation (appreciative inquiry), we change the energy of the entire conversation and open people up for the tough work that follows. That helps us get to an aspirational WHY and often to a strong WE.

The following summarizes how appreciative inquiry questions are different:

- The questions we ask, almost always determine the answers we get. Essentially, we live in the world our questions create.

- The more positive our questions, the easier it will be for us to conceive of positive and constructive outcomes.

- When we ask people to answer questions from a position of strength, we give them the opening and space to be the hero of our story. Ultimately, that's what helps people to see value in their joining our call-to-action.

- Our questions create the space for movement and change, if we ask them right. They should open up the space for people to reconsider their prior disposition – not because they were wrong, but because WE HAVE THE OPPORTUNITY to create something really great together! If our goal is to prove we're right and then, make others wrong, we remove the incentive and space for self-reflection and correction. This may seem counter-intuitive, but few people like to admit that they may have made an error in judgement and if you start there (what's wrong), it's unlikely to win the support you need to advance your work.

Below are some foundational appreciative inquiry questions for a variety of situations in which you are likely to be making a case. They are meant to be general examples but feel free to tailor ones that best reflect the uniqueness of your stakeholders and the context in which you are working.

Appreciative Inquiry Questions For People:
- What has been a high-point experience in your life when you felt most alive, successful, and effective?

- Without being humble, what do you value most about yourself, your work, and your organization?

- What can you continue doing to keep amplifying the good in your life and with people around you?

- What are the assets you bring or contribute to this community, city, or the region?

Appreciative Inquiry Questions For Organizations:
- What are the core factors that make this organization function at its best, when it feels like a great place to be in, and without which it would cease to exist?

- Imagine it is three years into the future and the organization is just as you would want it to be. What's happening that makes it vibrant and successful? What has changed? What has stayed the same, and how have you contributed to this future?

- What can you begin to do to move the organization in the direction of our greatest desires? What can you stop doing because it no longer serves the organization or because it gets in the way?

- What are some transitions you'll need to make because you have existing responsibilities and constraints, and can't just drop everything immediately?

- What is the part of the organizational theory of change / action that inspires you? How does your work in this organization and the expertise that you bring contribute to the heart of this organization?

Appreciative Inquiry Questions For Communities:
- When you think about the future of this city and your neighborhood in particular, what are you most optimistic about?

- You could live anywhere in the world or in the country, what makes you love this community? Not the parks and weather or cultural things like zoos, but other things that are really unique about this community that makes you excited to be here, even on a tough day.
- Have you been here long enough to remember when the people in this community were able to overcome a major issue? How did that happen? What made that successful?

- Wow, that's amazing! Sounds like people here have a proven track record of tackling tough problems and winning! How does it make you feel to know that people in this community overcame such a challenging issue in the past?

- Why do you think this is the right and perfect moment to be coming together to improve this community and address whatever challenges exist here?

- How can we take advantage of the opportunity in front of us to make this region/city/community better for everybody?

- As we look to make investments in our future, what do you think is the smartest investment we can make to improve this community?

- Since we decide our future, what decisions are you ready to make to improve this community!

The Smartest Investment We Can Make in Our Town's Future, is To Secure a Foundation of Strong Communities and Stable Homes.

·TRY ME!

Our Town is comprised of vibrant neighborhoods and a dynamic economy—built on livability and affordability—that gives us a strong competitive advantage, across the state and nationally. Our local businesses attract dedicated employees, our colleges recruit high-caliber talent, and our neighborhoods boast strong and welcoming communities.

This is a critical time to be investing in Our Town. Our Town is one of the few remaining places where housing remains relatively affordable in the state. The favorable Interest rates remain relatively low and growth prospects for the region are optimistic.

Expanding homeownership opportunities to more households across Our Town, not only helps more households build wealth but it enables mortgage lenders to redress redlining and other discriminatory practices that have stained the credibility of the finance industry for decades.

If we act now, we can stop the displacement that threatens to upend whole neighborhoods in Our Town - making it difficult for families to stay connected to the jobs, schools, community centers, arts and cultural events that they have come to love. No one thrives if we price out young adults who have the talent and skills to strengthen our businesses. No one thrives if businesses leave Our Town because they can't attract and retain a workforce. No one thrives if families struggle to put a roof over their heads.

But we all thrive when people who work here, have stable homes here. We all thrive when our work to bring more businesses and prosperity to Our Town, includes everybody. We all thrive when people see a future here and can raise their families stably here or start new business ventures here.

The more people succeed in Our Town, the more we lay the foundation for Our Town's future. We all have a stake in the success and stability of the neighborhoods that make up Our Town. They are the lifeblood and central arteries of our community. They fuel the engine of our economy. They nurture the diversity of our people and provide outlets to share culture, food, parks, festivals and more.

The neighborhoods in Our Town ensure our future – yours and mine! The smartest investment we could make together is uniting in policies that strengthen all neighborhoods across Our Town.

Every home, in every neighborhood should be a place where possibility, hopefulness, and opportunity thrive.

We will make Our Town better- block-by-block. Leaving the old practices of exclusion behind and leaning into laying a new foundation for strong and stable homes in every neighborhood in Our Town. Nothing less will do, because we have decided that we can do better!

# Principle #2: Name the Power of the Moment to Shape the Future

In this second principle, we need to highlight three things: *urgency, agency,* and *optimism*.

Get Urgency in the Conversation

Naming the importance of this moment is key to getting the attention and urgent action of your stakeholders. Your stakeholders are not living in an isolated bubble. They are responding to a wide variety of crises, adaptive challenges, issues, concerns and opportunities both in the present but also, those that they anticipate will come at some point in the future.

In most communities, there is a long list of challenges that leaders are trying to solve. It is easy for our issues to get pushed aside for other more pressing and immediate "crises". In some cases, there may be other critical priorities that your stakeholders need to solve first. However, the case for our work is made much stronger when those stakeholders come to understand the urgency of the moment in the issues we raise too.

You are more likely to get their attention when you connect the issue you are trying to solve with a bigger catalytic moment or an issue that is marked URGENT for your stakeholders! For example, a new transit system is being built in the region which could open doors for creating affordable housing or co-locating other community resources. A natural disaster may have recently happened (think COVID-19, wildfires, floods, hurricanes), prompting new resources to be delivered around community building and it may offer up the opportunity to think about resilience.

Those issues are top-of-mind for your stakeholders and are likely to be the issues that get attention fastest. If those urgent priorities are NOT specifically the thing that you are making a case to address, you need a strategy that positions your issue as urgent as well.

The fastest way to do that is to *"hitch your wagon"* to larger animating issues. That is, help people see how your issue is directly related to our ability to solve this other/larger set of issues. That way, it makes it easier for you to garner the attention and visibility you need with your stakeholders, and they won't see the attention you give to it as distracting.

The good news is that there are plenty of big challenges facing your stakeholders that are likely very relevant to the case you are trying to make.

Go ahead and identify the bigger catalytic moment on the horizon and draw the dotted line for your stakeholders, between their urgent moment (or one that is looming) and yours!

Be careful however not to drive the conversation with "crisis" talk. That is, don't let the urgency of the issues that you are working to resolve, push you into the crisis-oriented language that often pervades public conversation. Once upon a time, before the advocates on every major social issue used (and mis-used) the "language of crisis" to position their issue, that strategy might have worked. Today however, you will need to be a bit more creative and thoughtful in how you position the urgency of your issue, if you expect to elevate it on the long list of priorities for leaders. So those "crises" are opportunities to shape our future, opportunities to think bigger and more innovatively than we did in the past. That is, move the crisis talk out of your casemaking and move "forward thinking, planning" into your case for change.

Get Agency in the Conversation
Early on in our case, we must help people connect to their agency – to their power as decision-makers. This is important, in part because most people don't feel that they have any power to change the external conditions around them.

Most of us have become comfortable with the idea that others control our destiny – namely government. We typically assign all our social problems to "government", then rail against the fact that THEY haven't solved those problems. It's comfortable and convenient but it doesn't put people in the driver's seat of decision-making or social action.

So, our task in this principle is to put people in the driver's seat – reminding them that how WE act in this important moment makes all the difference. Reminding them of the times when average everyday people came together to do something powerful in your community, helps them to get in touch with their power and their sense of their own agency.

Put People in the Future
Finally, help people use their agency to think about your shared future. When people think about the future, they get much more optimistic about the life they can create – personally and with others in their community. Mobilizing people to create the future community they envision, helps get people energized for the tough work ahead. So, take the time to remind them that we have the power to shape the future we all desire AND the moment is now to start. When you make this part of your pitch, you help energize people, set in the future.

Reflection Questions

- Do I have a clear understanding of what big opportunities, fears or challenges my stakeholders are facing?
- What are the big adaptive challenges facing my stakeholders?
- Did I connect my issue with a trend, an event, an investment, or some other catalytic moment that my stakeholders are concerned with?
- Did I use my data or vivid stories to connect my issue with that catalytic moment?
- Did I provide examples of how a collaboration with my stakeholders would help connect to something on their strategic horizon?

Your Ticket to Implementing This Principle

Start by getting your stakeholders to think about the future. Pace them into the future by asking them to think about what they'd hope to see in the community within the next 10 to 15 years. Then ask them a series of follow-up questions to really make that vision come to life. Questions like – What does it feel like to live there? What does it smell like? What kind of shops or businesses are located there? Are kids playing there? What kinds of resources are in the community in the future to nurture the development of your young people? What things do you most enjoy in that future community?

Separately, take some time to have them think about what the adaptive challenges are – that is, what kinds of circumstances are we likely to face in the near future, that we'll need to prepare for (or adapt to) today. That is, what opportunities and challenges do we need to start preparing for today, so that our community has a brighter future?

Reflect on the "pain points" that are relevant for your stakeholders, if they don't start to prepare for that future. What are the issues they'll need to solve for and how does your solution help them to do that. Think carefully about who (besides you and your organization) NEEDS to solve the issues you've raised and help them to see how helping you, helps them, solve issues that are relevant and compelling for them.

Sample Success Measures

- **KPI #1 (urgency):** We are explicitly and consistently tying our issues to those that are already important priorities to our stakeholders.
- **KPI #2 (agency):** We are consistently reminding people of their own power to change the world.
- **KPI #3 (future orientation):** We are consistently positioning people in the future.

- **Outcome #1 (urgency):** Our stakeholders start to talk about this issue as if it solves a problem or pain point that THEY have; powerfully connecting this issue to priorities they already have.
- **Outcome #2 (agency):** Our stakeholders start to talk about the issue as their responsibility and within their power to solve.
- **Outcome #3 (future orientation):** Our stakeholders start to talk about this issue as part of a bigger, shared future they envision with us.

- **Impact #1 (urgency):** Our stakeholders see our issue as important to solving the issue they see as a chief priority as inextricably connected to their ability to solve THEIR problems (both present and future).
- **Impact #2 (agency):** Our stakeholders see solving the issue as their responsibility to solve.
- **Impact #3 (future orientation):** Our stakeholders see solving the issue as part of the way that we get to the bigger future that is possible for all of us.

FUTURE PACING: GETTING TO THE HEART OF THE FUTURE WE FACE TOGETHER

This is one of my favorite casemaking techniques – mostly because it is one of the easiest to master. The idea of future pacing is simple. When you give your stakeholders and strategic partners a window to the future, you put them in a stronger disposition to say yes to your call-to-action. Generally, people can be very cynical when you ask them to think about the current state of affairs. But when you ask them to vision forward or to picture the future they want, it puts them in a very different emotional state. It shifts the energy in the conversation, in their thinking and in their disposition.

This future orientation works in part because it gets people out of trying to explain what hasn't worked in the past and why things have "gotten so bad in the first place". When people look at problems as they exist today, few people want to volunteer to take responsibility for the part they might have played in how that problem emerged in the first place, but...the future is a different story. The future hasn't happened yet and is something that we can plan together and where people feel like they have some agency (or ability to influence what happens next), so they are more optimistic about whatever it is that you need them to do. **The future focus shifts us out of a conversation of trying to explain our failure (which inspires no one), to planning our future (which motivates action more effectively than talking about our current day crises or tough problems).**

Future pacing is not just a technique in casemaking. Psychologists use this technique in their work when they want to motivate their clients. They'll say something like, *"close your eyes and think about where you'd like to be in one year...then in two years...then in five years...then in ten years. Imagine what it will feel like to reach your goals in one year...then your two-year goal... then your five-year goal...then the ten."* Pacing people out into the future helps them to imagine living in a world in which the outcomes they've worked hard to achieve, actually come to fruition. It helps them to put their aspirations, hopes, and dreams into a vision and subsequently, to see beyond the problems of today.

Health practitioners and motivational coaches also use this technique when they are trying to motivate their clients to overcome the barriers to health and wellbeing. Doctors, for example, might use it on a patient who is reluctant to take blood pressure medication because the medication sparks hair loss or some other negatively perceived appearance issue. The doctor would ask the patient about what they are looking forward to in the future – perhaps a daughter's wedding, a new grandchild on the way, retiring from a job, or buying a new house – whatever it is, the doctor would then say, *"well the only way you're going to be around for that future is to make sure that you take this medication with regularity. Don't miss out on the most important day in your daughter's life, or kissing your grandchild for the first time, or enjoying your new life in retirement."*

The subtle art to future pacing is getting people to actually engage their intellect as well as their emotions. So, when they are imagining the future, ask them how they feel in that moment, what they see, what they smell, and to describe as much as they can about their vision. The more details they can offer, the more they own the vision as they see it (meaning the more they see themselves in it). Then ask them, who is helping them bring it to fruition – the community organizations, the businesses, the agencies, the friends, and family. That helps them to envision the future as a collective one that involves the competencies and contributions of many.

Future pacing is an especially good technique when you need to deliver bad news. Bad news can be any news that you expect to have a negative impact on people's inspiration to do the work that you need them to do. For example, when you have to deliver bad news about the steady rise in homelessness or your organization's shrinking budget, or any number of other challenging issues. To make the case that people continue to stay the course (if you've got good reason to think that is the wise course of action), pace them out a bit.

Say something like, "We are doing all we can to reduce homelessness in the region. We have a more aggressive set of policies and programs in place than ever before. But this challenge was not made in a day and it will not be solved in a day. It will take the steadfast resolution and commitment of this community over a number of years for us to make sure that every person in this region is safely housed, every night!

With the investments that we are making to tackle this issue, by 2030 we expect to see homelessness finally be a problem of the past. Our goal is to make homelessness a brief, rare, and non-recurring experience for people. And with your continued and steadfast support, despite the bumps in the road we are seeing, we can do this!"

The latter wouldn't be the only things that you might say but focusing the energy (and the data) on the future helps take the sting out of the early, unavoidable challenges of solving tough adaptive challenges.

A Message from the Future with Representative Alexandria Ocasio-Cortez

One of the most recent examples of future pacing comes from Representative Alexandria Ocasio-Cortez of New York in a video where she makes the case for the Green New Deal. In the video she asks, *"What if we actually pulled off a Green New Deal? What would the future look like? For the Green New Deal to become a reality we must be able to close our eyes and imagine it."*

The video opens with her in the future talking about the existence of a bullet train, in a future time where we've already been able to achieve the Green New Deal.

Here, I share selected passages from the video voiceover that Rep. Ocasio-Cortez provides. It is a clear example of this kind of future pacing.

Voiceover of Rep. Ocasio-Cortez:

"Ah, the bullet train from New York to D.C. It always brings me back to when I first started making this commute. In 2019, I was a freshman in the most diverse Congress in history up to that point. It was a critical time. I'll never forget the children in our community. They were so inspired to see this new class of politicians who reflected them, navigating the halls of power. It's often said, "You can't be what you can't see." And for the first time they saw themselves.

I think there was something similar with the Green New Deal. We knew that we needed to save the planet and that we had all the technology to do it. But people were scared. They said it was too big, too fast, not practical. I think that's because they just couldn't picture it yet. Anyways, I'm getting ahead of myself.

Let's start with how we got here...America became the biggest producer and consumer of oil in the world...

We lost a generation of time we'll never get back, entire species will never get back, natural wonders gone forever. And in 2017 Hurricane Maria destroyed the place where my family was from, Puerto Rico. It was like a climate bomb. It took as many American lives as 9/11. And in the next year when I was elected to Congress, the world's leading climate scientist declared another emergency. They told us that we had 12 years left to cut our emissions in half or hundreds of millions of people would be more likely to face food and water shortages, poverty, and death. Twelve years to change everything: How we got around, how we fed ourselves, how we made our stuff, how we lived and worked, everything.

The only way to do it was to transform our economy, which we already knew was broken since the vast majority of wealth was going to just a small handful of people and most folks were falling further and further behind. It was a true turning point. Lots of people gave up. They said we were doomed.

But some of us remembered that as a nation we'd been in peril before: the Great Depression, World War II. We knew from our history how to pull together to overcome impossible odds. And at the very least, we owed it to our children to try.

The way it began was that Democrats took back the House in 2018 and then the Senate and the White House in 2020. Then we launched the decade of the Green New Deal, a flurry of legislation that kicked off our social and ecological transformation to save the planet. It was the kind of "swing for the fence" ambition we needed. Finally, we were entertaining solutions on the scale of the crises we faced *without leaving anyone behind. That included Medicare for All, the most popular social program in American history.*

We also introduce the federal jobs guarantee, a public option including dignified living wages for work. Funny enough, the biggest problem in those early years was a labor shortage. We were building a national smart grid, retrofitting every building in America, putting trains like this one all across the country.

We needed more workers. That group of kids from my neighborhood were right in the middle of it all - especially this one girl, Ileana. Her first job out of college was with AmeriCore Climate, restoring wetlands and bayous in coastal Louisiana. Most of her friends were in her union, including some oil workers in transition. They took apart old pipelines but got to work planting mangos at the same salary and benefits.
Of course, when it came to healing the land, we had huge gaps in our knowledge. Luckily, indigenous communities offered generational expertise to help guide the way.

...Those were years of massive change, and not all of it was good. When Hurricane Sheldon hit southern Florida, parts of Miami went underwater

for the last time. But as we battled the floods fires and droughts, we knew how lucky we were to have started acting when we did. And we didn't just change the infrastructure. We change how we did things. We became a society that was not only modern and wealthy, but dignified and humane too. By committing to universal rights like healthcare and meaningful work for all, we stopped being so scared of the future. We stopped being scared of each other. And we found our shared purpose.

...When I think back to my first term in Congress riding that old school Amtrack in 2019 all of this was still ahead of us and the first big step was just closing our eyes and imagining it.

We can be whatever we have the courage to see."

Principle #3: Tell People What They Lose if They Sit on the Sidelines

On most social issues, when we poll Americans about their policy preferences, we typically see widespread support for a number of policies, programs, services and investments that are aligned with a much more compassionate response to the social problems we face. Wide majorities of Americans strongly favor a nationalized health care system where all of us have ready access to the health care we need, regardless of income. Wide majorities of Americans favor policies that would create more affordable housing for low- and moderate-income Americans. For examples, in many areas of the country, when community residents have the option at the ballot box to tax themselves to provide more resources for people experiencing homelessness – they do!

To have strong public opinion in favor of these issues is great but let's ask ourselves why aren't more people involved in the fight to make those policies the law of the land or to make sure that those opinions are carried out by corporations, government agencies, nonprofits and other institutions that play a role in the ecosystem that can make those outcomes happen?

Although public opinion may be on your side, getting people mobilized to participate in making those opinions a reality, is more challenging.

One part of this challenge is because of what we described in Principle #2, that many people do not have a strong sense of their own power to change the conditions around them. They believe only large institutions or big influencers (usually understood as wealthy Americans) can really make big structural changes happen. They don't have faith that their actions can be impactful or decisive. So, they sit on the sidelines and watch their futures be determined by others who have different interests and who see a different future for our nation.

A second cause to explain why people sit on the sidelines of justice is that they believe that they may lose more by getting involved, than by sitting it out. For example, if the issue is a better version of nationalized health care, people may believe that a new governmental approach to providing such care may result in even worse outcomes than they already have. They may fear that their costs will be driven up because of the change in health care policy. Fearing change and being more negatively impacted, they opt out of working toward a future that advances a way for all of us to have the health care that we need, at a price that is affordable.

Our task in this third principle is to give people a reason to get off the fence – a reason that is not baked in crisis language but rather is based on reminding them that there are larger consequences for sitting on the sidelines.

Highlight for your stakeholders, what will happen to your community – for them and for everybody else – if they choose to do nothing. If you are truly working on an important and compelling problem, it is likely that things would get much worse, if we continue to kick the can down the road. Powerfully communicate why immediate action gives us a better chance at solving the issue and call out the "adaptive leaders" who can see beyond the immediacy of today, toward the future we all deserve.

When you remind people that there are also consequences for doing nothing, it helps you defeat the inclination many people have to "wait and see". Point out examples of other communities that took a "wait and see" attitude and remind people of the opportunity to chart a different course of action. Remind them of the positive vision they have of the future and how that future will be lost if it has no one to carry the torch in that direction.

Remind them that the real "loss" would be to pass up the opportunity to make a real difference for our children and their children. We don't want to look back years from now and regret having chosen to "wait and see" on big issues like climate change, affordable housing, health care and the like.

Don't we all want to leave a legacy to the next generation of a better world? Well, let's not lose the opportunity to choose that outcome today! Let's look back at this moment years from now and say, "Wow, I'm so glad we got in front of that issue and solved it, so that our children and the next generation are in a much stronger position than we were. Our children shouldn't have to solve problems that we've kicked down the road."

Reflection Questions

- Did I make it clear that being bystander and sitting on the sidelines leads to big losses for everyone?
- Did I calculate the consequences of doing nothing and explain that doing nothing is much worse than leaning forward?
- Did I paint a picture of the consequences of inaction and alternatively, paint the picture of the positive consequences of action now?
- Have I shared examples of communities where the "wait and see" approach failed?
- Have I assessed what people in my community are afraid to lose and argued that their inaction makes those losses inevitable?

Your Ticket to Implementing This Principle

This is one of the most important places in your case to leverage your data. Using data to paint a picture of the consequences of inaction gives this part of your case stronger legs. Start with the positive data – what happens 10, 15, 20 years from now if we lean in and invest our resources to resolve this issue...then present the alternative (vividly and with pictures). What happens if this moment passes with no action, and we make no (or little) effort to change how we address this issue?

Sample Success Measures

- **KPI:** We are consistently using our data and narratives to show the two tomorrows – what happens if we intervene and what happens if we don't.
- **Outcome:** Our stakeholders are no longer debating WHETHER we need to act, they are debating on how soon we need to act and what shape those immediate actions will take. They have a more sober assessment of what is lost without action!
- **Impact:** Our stakeholders begin prioritizing this issue for immediate action - on the agenda of their meetings, in the programs they offer, the investments they make, and services they make available.

LOSS AVERSION &
THE PERCEPTION OF RISK

"If we could be freed from our aversion to loss, our whole outlook on risk would change."

Alan Hirsch

Loss aversion is a cognitive bias that we all have, and it simply says that the pain of loss (or perceived loss) is stronger than the joy of any gain (or perceived gain) we get from our actions. If we could draw the basic philosophy on the back of a napkin, it would look like this:

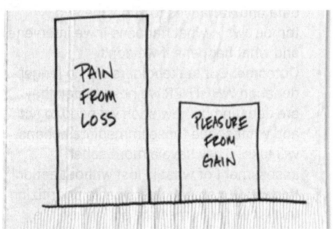

The idea was coined by legendary psychologists Amos Tversky and Daniel Kahneman out of their research in the early 90s and it is critical to understand human decision-making. Fear of loss (or people's perception of loss) is a big part of what shapes their decision-making. This fear is so powerful that Chris Voss, one of the world's expert hostage negotiators often refers to loss aversion as "bending reality", because loss aversion distorts people's perception so much that it literally – bends their perception of reality!

Why are we so afraid of losing? Our aversion to loss is a strong emotion. The aversive response reflects the critical role of negative emotions (anxiety and fear) to losses. In other words, loss aversion is an expression of fear. This explains why we tend to focus on setbacks rather than progress – even when progress has been greater than any setbacks. Negative emotions, such as from receiving criticism, have a stronger impact than good ones, such as from receiving praise.

Simply put, we HATE to think that we are losing (or could lose). When we feel like our support for policies like affordable housing, health care reform, climate change or any other major system reform, will net us a loss of ANY kind, we reject the possible gains that might work in our favor (and in favor of those around us). This is true even when the gains we're likely to have, far outweigh any loss we might suffer.

What's ironic is that on a lot of policy issues where people might experience gains (or improvements in their wellbeing or economic situation), they reject those policies for fear that somehow, they might have to give up, sacrifice, or lose something. And, as it turns out, most people are not very good at predicting what losses they would sustain or the magnitude of those perceived losses, in the first place. **So, the losses that people think they will sustain are rarely realistic or measured assessments of risk but typically represent their perceptions (magnified in abstract), which makes it almost impossible to get people to move forward when the perception of loss looms so large.**

The takeaway for the changemakers among us, is this - if you want to move people forward and to have them respond to your call-to-action, you must navigate this issue of loss aversion very strategically. You must get the perception of loss back on the other side of the table. That is, get people to think about what they will lose if they fail to work with you to change those outdated systems for the better.

If your intent is to move them forward, you must find out how they feel they are losing because that's going to be the single dominating factor in their decision-making. Often, their perceptions are not even rational, but you have to understand those perceptions, in order to bend them. Perception of loss is what keeps people up at night. Nobody gets insomnia because life is good, instead they stay up worrying at night when they think they're losing something! They come to community or city council meetings, ready to shout down policymakers because they fear losing something – rarely because they have a "thank you" to offer. It's never rational and it's always bent based on their perceptions.

And here is the trick. You must know what kinds of things they value so much that they are especially afraid to lose those things. Are they afraid to lose their health or the health of their loved ones? Is it fear that their children will not receive the advantages they need to do well in the economy that is coming? Is it fear that they will lose their economic security or their ability to retire with enough resources to be comfortable?

If you don't know what people are afraid to lose, you don't know what will motivate them to support your cause. So, find out! Ask them what they would be afraid to lose about their community? What are they optimistic about in for their own future? What are they looking forward to in the next 10 years and what (if anything) makes them excited about those upcoming years?

When you start to get underneath these questions, you'll have what you need to pull your stakeholders forward to support your cause. Connect your issue to the things that your stakeholders value most – the things they are most afraid to lose. And be clear about the ways in which, your call-to-action will help them avoid losing those things.

One caveat here should be noted: we never condone people holding onto bigoted or racist fears and our words should never enable them to do so. Sometimes people are holding onto things that are not conducive to the values of equity, fairness and inclusive communities. They may be holding onto bigoted practices, racialized policies that keep our communities divided or things like segregated neighborhoods, and they are afraid to lose those things. So, their perceptions of loss are connected to bigotry or racism or other outdated values.

If those are the things that people are afraid to lose, you need to do more digging. Usually if you dig underneath their bigoted or racist viewpoints, there lies a more basic fear. Fear that they won't belong to the new community practices that you are creating; fear that more equitable policies for all, will leave them behind; fear that they will lose what little control they have over their own lives or worse, fear that they will lose the power to control other people's lives!

Once you've identified what's underneath those viewpoints, you are in a much stronger position to unseat those views. In fact, you won't be able to unseat those views unless you can pinpoint the underlying fear.

Be clear from the outset, that you do not agree nor condone their bigoted or racist viewpoints. State that unequivocally and do not hedge on that (i.e., *I appreciate your concerns, but I do not support any policies that undermine people's dignity, worth, humanity or sense of belonging to this community*).

Then connect their underlying fears back to the importance of the work you are trying to do (i.e., *So you are afraid this community will change and bring more people of color, well you should be more afraid that without exposure to a diversity of people, your children will be unprepared for the economy and the jobs that are coming. Those jobs will need people who can adapt easily to people of different races, faiths, background, gender identity, sexual orientation and more.*

Those jobs will require that people have some fluency and effectiveness in engaging people

*from all socio-economic levels. It's such a shame
that your choices are leaving your children so
unprepared for the jobs of the future. Even with so
much education and training, they are likely to be
left behind by a world that is changing and
diversifying rapidly. That's especially a shame
when you compare so many other communities
who are using the diversity of their communities to
prepare their children for bright and prosperous
futures. The jobs of the future are waiting for those
children, but it looks like they will leave yours
behind*).

Perhaps your example would be less direct than
mine above and more tailored to the specific issue
in your community or sector. But whatever it is, be
clear that you'll need to explicitly put "loss" on the
other side of the table. Be clear how people are
losing out because they are delaying action on this
issue and that those delays have costly
consequences. When we do that, we can "*bend
their reality*" back in our favor and put urgency
back where it belongs.

We cannot change the fact that fear motivates
action faster (and more profoundly) than the
expectation of gain. But we do have some control
over how we help balance out those fears –

getting perceptions of loss back where they belong. Master this principle and you'll be able to navigate a huge impediment to action.

TRY ME! No One Should Be Required to Demonstrate Odds-Defying Resilience to Live. We Need Our Health Delivery Systems to Work Better

Can you imagine your community without its primary resources for wellness? Or, without the ability to deliver preventative and emergency care when you need it most?

Well, if we fail to invest in improving our health delivery system, you won't have to imagine it. You may be forced to live it.

As the spread of the COVID-19 virus has made painfully clear, our country needs to rethink how we deliver health care and prevent the spread of infectious diseases. Today as this deadly virus threatens to upend our entire way of life, there is new urgency in rethinking that system.

We have not built up an efficient system for handling health crises at the scale of what we are witnessing with COVID-19 and public health experts warn that eventually, we will likely need to battle multiple health crises simultaneously. No one wants to be told that their hospital simply has no more beds or that their deceased loved ones have been stashed in a refrigerated truck outside because there is no more room for them in the hospital (as some people were made to experience during our worst COVID-19 outbreak).

Every day that we fail to act affirmatively to prepare our health system for the worst-case scenarios, makes us more ill-prepared when those scenarios start to play out. Every day spent without the resources, investments, and innovations necessary to improve our health delivery system, leaves us all in jeopardy.

When our health care professionals must spend their time wading through outdated practices, policies, equipment, or institutional arrangements, to deliver care, nobody wins. We all lose.

As we rethink how health care is delivered and funded, it is unlikely that there will be any one person, one organization, one agency, or one company that will provide the complete solution, so our work must be a collaborative effort. This work requires outstanding leadership and for us to be aware that what we're aiming to do is really, really hard on a ridiculously accelerated time scale.

We need to work as hard as we can collectively and as fast as we can. No one wants a repeat of the costly missteps during the early days of the spread of the COVID-19 virus, so we must focus.

We must assess where our systems are strong, where they lack the necessary supports, and then, forge a new pathway that makes them even stronger. We must use this moment to get serious about what it means to adapt our current health delivery system to the world that we have inherited. Not just to address the current COVID-19 pandemic but for the next one already on its way.

Let's choose to be prepared for the next one!

Principle #4: Navigate the Dominant Narratives

It would be so much easier to make our case if our stakeholders were blank slates – that is, they didn't already have opinions about how the world works, stereotypes, biases, and misinformation that limited their ability to see a brighter future. Unfortunately, this is not the circumstance in which we find ourselves. Often, our stakeholders have already formed opinions about the issues we are trying to solve, opinions about the relevance and importance of those issues, as well as judgements about the deservedness of the people they think will benefit from our solutions.

While some of those pre-existing beliefs are constructive, the narratives that tend to dominate our public policymaking are not always helpful for those of us trying to reimagine how our systems can produce more equity, more justice. This is because the dominant narratives in our nation tend to mirror, justify, and reinforce the status quo. At the institutional level, dominant narratives can sound like this, *"but we've always done it this way"*, *"we have too much at stake to take this risk"*, or *"the private market is more efficient than the government"*, *"that's not our role"* or *it'll cost more"* or *"it's too much change, too fast"*.

At the level of broader public narratives, dominant narratives can sound like this, *"if you help them, they'll just become more dependent on government"*, *"those people don't deserve to be helped"* or *"everyone has an individual responsibility to take care of their own families, don't ask me to pay for somebody else's failure"*.

Our task is not to try to talk people out of these dominant narratives – that strategy is rarely successful and usually backfires (pushing people more staunchly in support of stereotyped beliefs and biases). Making our case requires us to carefully either reframe the conversation or pivot entirely, to more productive ways of thinking about the issue.

Let's be clear about one thing however – **shifting, navigating, or pivoting around a dominant narrative is NOT the same thing as casemaking.** Rather, narrative shifting work can help support your casemaking because it helps you avoid triggering the opinions, misperceptions, stereotypes, and bias that can negate understanding of the solutions you are proposing in your case.

Reflection Questions
- Do I know what dominant narratives are pushing me into backfire territory when I try to make my case?
- Have I identified the preexisting beliefs and dominant narratives that shape public opinion about my issue?
- Have I avoided triggering the dominant narratives that reduce support for the case I am making about that issue?
- Have I developed a reframing or pivoting strategy to unseat harmful dominant narratives and am I using those strategies consistently to better connect to my stakeholders?

Your Ticket to Implementing This Principle

Your task is to skillfully navigate the dominant narratives. If the dominant narratives are deeply held beliefs, then your best bet is to reframe away from those narratives entirely. If those narratives are distracting but not deep-seated belief systems, you'll have an easier time pivoting around them.

In either case, being able to assess what's being triggered as you make your case, is essential to win stakeholder support. Your task is not to change the subject or avoid tackling the big issues or biases you see, but by reframing or pivoting, you are buying yourself some time by getting people who would otherwise easily avoid the conversation, to listen.

Think of it as "relabeling" – the same practice that designer retailers use when they want you to buy something that you wouldn't have purchased when it was priced 100 times over their costs! If they can do it, so can you!

Sample Success Measures

- **KPI:** We are consistently pivoting away from the dominant narratives to ones that avoid harmful backfires.
- **Outcome:** Our stakeholders are also moving away from those dominant narratives (engaging less in stereotypical/biased conversations on this issue) and beginning to use our new narratives.
- **Impact:** We have unseated the dominance of harmful narratives associated with this issue, in favor of more positive ones.

TO PIVOT OR REFRAME – THAT IS THE QUESTION

"That's such an interesting question, but as I listen to you, I think there's an even more interesting question for us to consider...

The ability to pivot from the conversation on the table, to the one you want to have, is one of the most important casemaking techniques to have in your toolbelt. If you've ever watched two good debaters go at it, I'm sure you've seen the fine art of an effective pivot. To pivot literally means to take a conversation topic that might be on a specific subject and move it to answer it on your own terms. That is, shifting the conversation back to a frame or a storyline that is consistent with the case that you are making. Think of this casemaking technique as helping your stakeholders and strategic partners stay focused on the mission, stay focused on what's important, stay focused on your call-to-action.

Pivots are a critical part of casemaking efforts because no matter how thoughtful we are in crafting our case, dominant narratives and negative disruptors are commonplace.

Dominant narratives are common societal narratives that reinforce ways of thinking that make it more difficult for people to see their collective interest in having systems designed for equity. For example, someone might say, *"yes I know that people need health care insurance, SO they should get a job that offers health care, buy it on the marketplace, or figure out how to get health insurance on their own."* That's the dominant narrative of individual responsibility talking and because of the repetition through which it is retold, that kind of narrative is hard to overcome for those trying to advance new policy models for expanding access to health care.

There are two types of dominant narratives – ones that are deeply held as part of our core belief system and those are not. The latter we simply call – negative disruptors. While they may dominate the conversation, they aren't so firmly affixed to people belief system that they can't be uprooted easily.

Think of the difference between your attempts to uproot an oak tree (something likely to have deep roots across a wide space) versus uprooting a tulip plant. The tulip plant is likely to require a handheld gardening tool and just a couple minutes versus the oak tree which may take professional tree removers, specialized equipment and more than a couple minutes, to uproot. As a result, we treat negative disruptors (our tulip plants) a bit more passively than we might other kinds of dominant narratives.

Negative disruptors can be equally harmful to our casemaking but the work to dislodge them is much easier. Negative disruptors tend to show up as statements of resignation that can deflate people's excitement about leaning forward.

For example, a typical disruptor in conversations about policy responses to homelessness often looks like this, *"those people are all drug addicts and they'll never be able to be positive contributors to our community."* This person may not be trying to enroll you in a belief system, but the comment is meant to dampen any bright ideas that you might have about creating new policies, programs, services, or investments for people experiencing homelessness. No matter what issue you are talking about, there will always be negative disruptors or statements made with the explicit purpose to shut down the aspiration to find better solutions.

So, we must be strategic in navigating around them!

Dominant Narratives

are common explanations, beliefs or ways of thinking that get reinforced through culture (*i.e. through the stories we tell and our cultural norms*) that make it more difficult for people to see their collective interest in having systems designed to produce equitable outcomes. Because dominant narratives are so normalized through their repetition and authority, they have the illusion of being objective and apolitical, when in fact they are neither.

REQUIRES

A Reframe Strategy

Negative Disruptors

often function like dominant narratives in that they can disrupt calls for collection action around equity and they get circulated through culture. What distinguishes negative disruptors is that they are not tightly held beliefs but rather, they are *statements of resignation* about the possibility of change. When people start to plan on the future they aspire to, negative disruptors function as reminders that social change is impossible, the battle for equity is a fool's errand and selective examples of how/when our past efforts to create social change have failed.

REQUIRES

A Pivot Strategy

More specifically, if our goal is to keep our stakeholders and strategic partners focused on the case we're making, we have to understand how to reframe a conversation as well as to master the fine art of the pivot. That means taking the dominant narrative or negative disruptors that you've been handed and turn that conversation right back around to the issues that you know matter. The better your reframe or pivot strategy, the more likely you are to keep your audience focused.

For example, we might reframe a conversation about affordable housing or addressing disparities in health (both topics that can engender a lot of opposition because of dominant narratives). We might begin the conversation about how we can ensure that our zip codes do not determine our access to a better life. We could share how people's outcomes differ across zip codes and ask our stakeholders if they believe that our zip code should have that much power over our lives. When we do that, we are essentially getting at the same problems, but people may not have the same defenses up or pre-existing stereotypes about "zip codes" as they do about "affordable housing" or "health equity".

A Reframe Strategy

Reframing a conversation means taking a different route to get to your destination (i.e., the

solution you are proposing as part of your case).
Think of reframing as putting the end goal or
destination into your GPS or navigation system.
The route guidance you get is likely to show you
multiple routes to get to that destination. One
route may take you directly through traffic, adding
hours more to your journey. Another route on the
GPS may take you in a totally different direction
but because there is no traffic on that pathway,
you'll get to your destination much faster. So, a
reframe strategy means looking at different routes
to get your audience to the destination (your
solution) AND AVOIDING THE TRAFFIC!

For example, rather than starting a conversation
about new early child development policies by
talking about the perils of low-income children
being underserved in our schools (a start that is
likely to backfire), you might start by talking about
the prosperity of our nation and how that
prosperity is dependent on our ability to nurture
the next generation of leaders. Empirical data
suggests that people are much more willing to
support new early child development policies
when we bring them into the conversation thinking
about what our nation needs to prosper versus the
specific needs of young children.

That may seem somewhat counter-intuitive but

empirical data says, you'll deliver more of your community stakeholders into the arms of more resources if your strategy routes people away from the dominant narratives about the perils of children and the schools they attend, and toward a narrative that lifts their aspirations to see a more prosperous nation.

Once you identify what dominant narrative is problematic, your reframing strategy needs to understand how to get to the destination by going a different route. That's a reframe strategy in a nutshell.

A Pivot Strategy

We've all engaged in the pivot at one point, whether we realize it or not. The good news is that there are examples everywhere – from the board room in business, to politics on the cable news channels, to your loved ones at home.

Here's an example from my personal collection!

Me (to my 11-year-old son): *Hey buddy, have you done your homework?"*

My son: *"Hey mom, I love you so much. What's for dinner?"*

Who can argue with a kid who starts a sentence with "I love you"! His homework did get done but he managed to buy himself time with that one. Some pivots are more effective than others but let's be clear, our ability to pivot determines a large part of how we're received.

Take the case of Lance Armstrong (the professional cyclist who found himself in the middle of a doping scandal). When he was asked about using drugs to enhance his performance in competitive cycling (before proof was available), he was able to pivot, buying him some necessary time to think about how he'd handle the situation. Though it didn't come in the form of an interview, interviewers were talking for years about his almost supernatural performance on the bike and hinting that it might be because of drug related enhancements.

Interviewers to Lance Armstrong:
    "What are you on?"

Lance Armstrong (his reply via his Nike Commercial):
    "What am I on? I'm on my bike busting my ass six hours a day. What are YOU on?"

Armstrong was able to use humor and a bit of bravado to push back on claims that tarnished his image (although we should note that eventually those claims were found to be true)!

The point here is that he was able to pivot to the conversation HE WANTED TO HAVE, which was about the sport he loved and how hard he was working to stay relevant in it. While I don't condone the dishonesty in his action and what he was covering up, the way in which he understood how to pivot is an interesting case study.

Armstrong's case reminds us that, as with everything else in this world, pivots can take both good and bad forms—and are put into play for strategic reasons. But how often have you been in a situation where you wanted to have a productive conversation about an issue but the people you were talking to were stuck in another frame? Or they were pushing back on your ideas using narratives that were totally unhelpful, misinformation or "alternative facts" – possibly even, lies? Or perhaps, they were stuck in a bedtime story (as we defined it earlier in this book) and they weren't able to hear your position because they couldn't shake their own pre-conceived notions?

There are indeed some people for whom, having you share your facts, data and evidence to the contrary helps them to see your point of view. Unfortunately, it is more often the situation that you'll have to either navigate around those unproductive perceptions or simply acknowledge what you have in common and pivot back to safer territory. So, mastering the fine art of pivoting is essential.

The good news is that the dominant narratives and negative disruptors are pretty predictable – rarely are people creative enough or interested enough to come up with entirely new disruptive things to say every time they meet you! Their lack of creativity and predictability gives us the opportunity to develop (and practice) a standard way that we'll pivot around the issues they raise.

Here are a couple ground rules about effective pivoting.

(1) **NEVER, EVER repeat back the unproductive information – even to clarify.** When you repeat back the negative things you've heard, you simply give your audience another opportunity to hear the other point of view...again! Refuse to entertain the unproductive information – especially if it

reinforces dominant narratives, negative stereotypes, bias or bigotry.

(2) **Don't spend much time trying to refute negative narratives or bogus claims/disruptors either.** Most negative disruptors aren't really talking about deep-seated issues they have in opposition to you. They are most likely using other issues or narratives as defensive shields, to avoid having a real or productive conversation about the issues that you are raising. So, it isn't a good use of your time to try to refute much of what they are raising as concerns, and it rarely helps when you do. You are on stronger ground if you go back to your own narrative, reinforce the values that you are upholding and work to educate people who are receptive (new champions) about why your solution is the best course of action for our future.

(3) **Learn the difference between a defensive pivot and an offensive one.** There are two kinds of pivots –the goal of one version is to defend ourselves against unfair or untrue characterizations (defensive – similar to what Armstrong did in our previous example), while the goal of the

second one is to actively move the conversation away from oppositional narratives back onto ones that are more productive (offensive). Practice using both so that when you're hit with a negative disruptor, you already know how to make the play (defensively or offensively) that allows you to get back to your own casemaking.

(4) **To pivot, use a bridging statement to find something that you can agree about and then, pivot back to your own narrative.** So, the best pivots tend to be those where you acknowledge something in common or some part of the other person's statement that you agree with, and then move back onto your narrative or frame. You are not required to agree with their arguments, but you can always find that one small idea, concern or nugget that you share in common. You might share your concern with the health of the community, or the accountability to our systems, or the wellbeing of our seniors. If that's all you can muster, go there first!

Some examples of bridging statements:

- *"I share your concern for our community, that's why I believe..."*
- *"Yes, about 10 years ago I would have said the same thing but here's what changed how I see this...*
- *"Thank you for saying that, it reminds me that..."*
- *"I can see how you could come to that opinion given your concerns, but the bottom line is that..."*
- *"You put a number of important issues on the table but what it all comes down to is this...."*
- *"Well I remember that happening as well, but my recollection suggests that...."*
- *"Yes, you've given a lot of information. What people really need to know though is that..."*
- *"Yes, those are important concerns, but we find the more troubling concern has to do with..."*

(5) **Practice the way that you'll pivot with others so that there is consistency in the alternative direction that you are setting.** Develop and practice a consistent pivot with other advocates so that together, you begin to rewrite the story, change the narrative, and rewrite the way that people see the issue over time.

Here's another example of a good pivot: When he was campaigning for health care reform, then President Barack Obama and his team made a number of strategic pivots to navigate around the negative disruptors in the public debate. Opposers of the legislation argued that people would lose their ability to choose their own physician as well as access to their existing health plans.

President Obama's pivot looked like this: *"If you like your health care plan, you can keep your health care plan. But under this plan, those same insurers will never be able to deny you coverage for a pre-existing condition if you change plans."*

First, he acknowledged something he could agree with and then, Obama would talk excitedly about pre-existing conditions – an issue where public support was rock solid, so he knew he was on solid ground.

If you want to advance a strong case for change, get a strong reframe strategy and master the art of the pivot! That's the way to keep people focused on your story telling.

`•TRY ME!` The Power of An Address

A bit of context for this example: The dominant narratives and negative disruptors around homelessness are toxic, making it difficult for solutions to gain traction. Pivot to a shared/common experience that reinforces the notion that people without shelter need the same things as everyone else: an address and the stability that it offers.

Washington, DC is one of the most prosperous and vibrant cities to live in the U.S. and home to many of the most powerful addresses in the world. Yet in the shadows of the White House, the Capitol buildings, national monuments, 175 embassies, luxury condominiums, upscale retail and restaurants, many of our neighbors do not have a home with an address to call their own.

Having an address is powerful—whether you are a world leader, a business owner, or a childcare worker. An address is required to register to vote, to enroll your children in school, to get a government I.D. or to apply for a job, to file any kind of government claim, and so much more. Research tells us that an address, a place to call home, provides us with so much more than the actual house number conveys — a sense of belonging, a connection to community, the ability to plan for the future, better health and job options.

While the region is home to a multitude of powerful addresses, far too many people in our region lack stable access to one. Often nestled between our high-profile addresses – the embassies, the monuments, the museums and the transit corridors – are tents that have become makeshift shelter to an increasing number of people who are locked out of the opportunity that an address provides.

Far too many of our neighbors lack the power of an address. They live in tents and sleeping bags in our parks and along our streets. Even more line up nightly to sleep in emergency shelters. Thousands more are living in unstable and often unsafe housing circumstances. Many of us know someone—a cousin, a friend, an employee—who is teetering on an edge so razor thin that any unforeseen event, expense, or challenge would put them in the street.

Despite the dire statistics about homelessness in our region, there is some good news to share. First, we are not alone. In fact, a small cadre of cities across the country are solving this issue by working together in multi-sector collaboration to redesign the systems that were meant to address the housing needs of their residents.

It is our turn now and the time is right. It is our time for our city to join a growing list of regions across the country that are tackling the issue of homelessness and winning. In a region as prosperous as ours, with so many prominent leaders and some of the wealthiest addresses in the world – we can and must do better. This should not be our reality and it cannot become our new normal.

Our work will ensure that everyone who lives here, no matter the circumstance, has the power of an address.

Join us! Add your address to our database of local champions who are ready to make sure that all of our neighbors have an address.

# **Principle #5:** Anchor and Credential Solutions, Not Problems

Let's start from a basic tenet of the world we live in today: data, statistics, and facts rarely win arguments. There was a time when many of us believed that if we had the right data and could share them at just the right moment (as new policies or programs were being debated, for example), we could win the day. There may still be some remnants of that lingering in the far reaches of public policy but generally, few real-world debates or arguments are won based on data we share. And almost none are ever won by positioning negatively framed, problem-centric data. That's bad news for many of us because "bad news data" has been the bread and butter of issue advocates for decades.

I remember as a young girl watching the movie, The Wiz. It was a soulful rendition of the Wizard of Oz, and it featured the singers Diana Ross and Michael Jackson – so it was a must see for me as a kid! There is one part of the movie when the Wicked Witch of the East sings a song warning her subjects not to bring her any bad news.

It was one of the scariest scenes in a movie that

my parents would allow me to watch and perhaps because of that, the images and song always stayed with me.

What about you? How often do you wake up in the morning craving to hear more bad news? If you're like me (and like the Wicked Witch of the East), bad news about the world around us is NOT what wakes you up in the morning and gets you ready to take on the world.

Yet so much of the data, messaging and engagement strategies used in the issue advocacy space, focus us on a steady diet of crisis and problem oriented, bad news stories. That diet demoralizes the same people and stakeholders that we want to engage and mobilize to action. Those types of negatively framed data stories don't really serve to get people motivated to lean forward to create real change in the world around us. Rather, those kinds of data stories just result in more of the blame game – complaining and pointing fingers at who is to blame for the state of our problems!

The availability of more data (especially data about the problems we face) has made it easier to tell these crisis-oriented stories – enabling us to credential those stories with a barrage of negatively framed facts and figures. We typically leave the more inspiring conversation about our solutions, to the end of our casemaking and sometimes, we fail to offer up concrete statistics and data to anchor support for the actions we want our stakeholders to take up.

To leverage the data we have, in support of effective casemaking, our task is to engage people in the bigger aspirations that our solutions provide and to do that BEFORE we launch into a conversation about problems. When we anchor people in solutions (especially those solutions that are future-oriented), we offer people the opportunity to be excited about the future that we can create together and our data lives in support of that future.

When we use our data to credential solutions, we invite our stakeholders to think with us about how to bring that future into existence and we release them from being stuck in the quicksand of today's problems.

Be clear though, this does not mean that we shouldn't talk about the problems and offer up sobering statistics, it just means that we do not START the conversation there. **Data are powerful if we use them in the right way – in support of solutions focused stories that anchor people in the strengths of who we are and the systems that need to be reimagined to manifest change.**

Reflection Questions

- Did I use my data to anchor my stakeholders in solutions, systems and our strengths or, did I use the data simply to default back to a conversation about our problems?
- Did I position the solutions as credible, achievable, forward-thinking, and feasible?
- Did I provide data examples of where the solutions or systems changes have worked in other places, to overcome the cynicism of negative disruptors?

Your Ticket to Implementing This Principle

There are two types of data. One type helps us to understand the magnitude and scope of the problems we need to solve; this type also helps us plan programs and investments. The other type of data inspires our stakeholders to action because they are genuinely excited about what is possible. The challenge is that we are often using the former, when we should be using the latter. Data-driven stories about how many people are poor, or hungry, or sick, or homeless (you name it), rarely gets people inspired. So, take the data you have and think about how you would present that information in a way that would inspire someone to lean forward or, collect new data that helps you tell a solutions-oriented story.

Sample Success Measures

- **KPI:** We are consistently using our data to tell solutions focused, systems based, and strength-oriented stories that inspire people about the future we can create together.
- **Outcome:** Our stakeholders are using our data to talk more about solutions, systems, or strengths rather than problems.
- **Impact:** Our stakeholders are solutions, systems, and strengths focused; they are excited about the solutions we proposed, and they use our data to credential those solutions.

MASTERING THE TECHNIQUES OF ANCHORING AND SOCIAL MATH

One of the most important and powerful casemaking strategies for leveraging data is a persuasive technique called *anchoring*. Attorneys, mediators, salespeople, and other skilled communicators often use this strategy to intentionally direct a conversation and enlist greater support for specific outcomes.

Anchoring responds to the human tendency to give the most weight to the first piece of information or idea provided to us when making decisions. Given this cognitive bias, it is essential that, when making a case for change, we choose the first piece of information or data—as our anchor—strategically. The data you use literally "anchors" people's thinking, so our task is to use the data that invites and encourages a positive response to our call-to-action.

Over the last twenty years, the amount of data we have access to has literally exploded. If all I knew about you was from the data I could collect from your cell phone, laptop, online profiles, and your credit card statements, I could almost write your life story! At least, the outlines of your story!

Yes, data is ubiquitous and the opportunity to use the data we're collecting about the state of our communities, our economy, our environment, our health, our homes, and much more, can be crucial in our casemaking.

Unfortunately, the way that most of us are using the data at our disposal doesn't often help our casemaking. We often start with negatively framed data that demoralizes people (reminding them of a whole lot of problems that seem too big to solve and totally out of their control), rather than exciting and engaging them about what is possible. For example, how many of us working on health equity issues start our appeals for support with something like this – *"the leading cause of death in this county for young people aged 7 to 14 is ____"* or *"the growing rate of ____ in our state, is cause for deep concern."* Not very inspiring is it and it actually feels depressing and overwhelming!

And for those of us looking to foster stronger support for racial equity work, we often start with a statement like this, *"...the rates for Black and Latinx populations are two times the rate for other groups – which is a serious cause for alarm".* This is alarming and important data, for sure but it backfires on us consistently (*i.e., "what's wrong with those people" or "why can't they function like everybody else"*).

While the severity and urgency of the problems we face may have brought you and your partners to the table, talking about problems typically does not get people excited about joining an effort to change systems. In fact, a good body of research in the cognitive sciences consistently finds that our brains are wired for optimism—which means anchoring your case in problems makes it likely that your potential stakeholders will disengage.

Yes, this information is relevant and important, to be sure. It helps us to describe the shape and dimension of the problems we are trying to solve. We are able to point out where there are gaps to be closed, alarming trends to be aware of, and where our interventions might best be targeted. In every possible way, these data are critical as we work to develop innovative and impactful solutions that drive health improvements in our communities.

The challenge here is that leading with negatively framed stats, like the examples above (as important as they are), is that they can make it harder to make the case. Negatively framed data may tell us more about the problem, but it also depresses our sense of engagement, agency, and optimism about solving those problems.

More important perhaps, these data tell us little about the possibilities for fixing those problems and does more to credential the problem, than the potential solutions. As a result, in most communities, people can tell you so much more about the problems they face than any of the feasible or recognized solutions to those problems.

They rail about what's wrong, because they have great practice in reciting narratives about what's wrong, but they are often totally unaware of the solutions that already exist (sometimes in their own backyards) and the support those solutions need to scale. When we probe people about what solutions they'd like to see enacted, more often than not we either get blank stares or some default back to what the problems.

Then, the backfires come along. Our stakeholders then default back to the familiar dominant narratives that feel like common sense to them. Often the dominant narratives about our "personal responsibility" end up displacing the solutions we had hoped to gather support for, and the problem is then pushed back on the very people who have not been well-served by our existing systems.

While people should be exercising "personal responsibility" in their own lives, odds-defying resilience should never be our metric of success. We need our systems to work better! Starting with problem-centric data starts this cascade of negativity that dead ends with the blame game rather than the outcomes we need.

We know that data is important, but the point is that unless we are clear about its role in how we make our case, we will use it in a totally counter-productive way. That is, our sense that data is important for equitable systems change is not misguided – data matter – but the importance of using those data strategically to strengthen how people receive our calls-to-action, is what needs our intentional rethinking.

Let's get specific about some of the ways the anchoring technique can help us leverage our data and strengthen the case we are trying to make. Here are general rules of thumb you can use to better manifest the power and potential of your data in your casemaking!

Use Your Data to Anchor People in Systems Thinking! Often, we use data to demonstrate the size, magnitude, and intensity of the problems we hope to solve. But, when we use data on the "front end" in this way, we essentially credential the problem and verify the need. So, instead, reinforce your case for systems-level change by using your data to anchor the systems-level solutions or approach that you are proposing.

If your goal is ultimately to change systems, you'll need to anchor people in systems level thinking right away. That means choosing a data point that reminds people of the systems we need to change. So, at the most basic level, anchoring a case for systems change means starting with systems-level data first and then consistently reinforcing and directing attention back to the need to change those systems. The more firmly you anchor data at the systems-level, the more likely it is that the resulting conversation among stakeholders will stay focused on systems change and your stakeholders will actually have the conversation you need them to have.

Here's an example: Many people in the affordable housing industry often make the case for change by highlighting how much individual renters or homeowners are paying for rent or mortgages (what they call, housing cost burdened). Because of their strong advocacy, an increasing number of Americans now understand that housing is a problem. That's the good news. The challenge is that most Americans have little understanding of the housing delivery system and what the constraints are for creating or preserving more affordable housing. So, the only level in which they can engage this conversation is at the level of consumption – i.e., "housing as a consumer good".

We know that this narrative of "housing as a consumer good" is a dominant narrative with a huge backfire in the public discourse! If we want to change the conversation, we've got to change the way we use our data. A better way forward is to highlight solutions that might make the housing delivery systems work better and more equitably in our communities. That's a systems issue!

In the chart below, housing advocates in one state shared results from a regional housing survey of development and construction professionals that highlighted the roadblocks they face as they try to produce more affordable housing. What is helpful to note here in the presentation of this data is that those roadblocks are presented as opportunities and as necessary investments to move affordable housing production forward, faster.

More than anything else, they suggest that our ability to improve the workforce in the housing sector would be one of the strongest investments policymakers could make to elevate capacity.

How Do We Ensure More Affordable Housing Gets Built?
Strong Investments in Housing Production Can Help

45%
Improving
Regulatory
Processes

76%
Improving
Labor
Supply

56%
Lowering
Cost of
Materials

By talking about the need for affordable housing in terms of the opportunities to improve the labor supply – it forces people to think about this issue at the systems level, in addition to the specific individual outcomes on people. We might follow up this chart with another showing how the investment in improving labor supply will help improve the cost of housing for renters and homeowners across the region. Focusing on labor supply might help us also position the issue of workforce development for the population of people likely to need affordable housing (that would be a 2-for-1, win-win).

Together, those data make a more effective case because it anchors people first in the systems that need rethinking – the housing delivery system and workforce development system, for starters. It then allows us the space to connect those systems back to the ultimate impact we hope to have. Starting with systems-level data allows us to show how those changes would transform the dynamic on the ground for a wide variety of community residents who desperately need more affordable housing options.

But we wouldn't be able to get people there if we started this conversation talking about how much people pay for rent or for mortgages. We'd certainly get their attention, but ALL of that attention would then be focused on whether those renters and homeowners were "managing their finances" rather than on how we change systems so that they work better. If we want people to lean forward in a call-to-action that is about systems change, then a great way to use our data is to anchor people there, right from the beginning!

Use Your Data to Help People See the Wider Range of Community Stakeholders that Touch (or Contribute to) the Solutions We Need. Most people have no idea how many government agencies, corporations, nonprofits, community-based organizations and residents are actually involved in any given policy issue or outcome that shapes their own community. Government is always the visible target but if you really want to change systems so that they work better for everyone, it's likely that you'll need to involve a wide range of people and institutions to make that happen.

Here's the challenge – how do you help the whole eco-system see their role in the solutions that you're asking for, when the only data you have in your hands is solely about the individuals who need help. There is a reason why the phrase "it takes a village is so popular". Well, if it takes a village, your data need to remind people of exactly who the village is, and what you need them to do.

In our last example the relationship between the housing delivery system and the workforce development system is a case in point. They are not things that average Americans tend to think about very much but the relationship between them determines in large measure, the cost and availability of the homes we live in.

So, we need people to better understand how systems work (or could be functioning differently, more efficiently and more equitably), else they can't fully lean forward in giving us the support we need from them.

Sometimes too we take for granted that people who work in your industry or sector can see "the village". Well, that's a wrong assumption. Even people who work in the sector may only see their part of the work but not see the overall village. So, it's up to you to get the data that can support this acknowledgement.

The data you need here can take many forms – data on how the regulatory processes (i.e. red tape); data on the lack of coordination within a system or across stakeholders; or data on the workforce and the time it takes to prepare job seekers for those jobs. The important point to make here is that your stakeholders need to see a wider range of stakeholders and policy levers for change.

Here's an example: We'll stick with housing as an example here. Affordable housing is actually a great example because most people have no idea how affordable housing is created, built or preserved. The enormous work that it takes to finance affordable housing or to place it in neighborhoods (avoiding the not-in-my-backyard attitudes), the regulations placed on housing developers, or the impact fees associated with such developments and much more. In fact, the "to-do" list for affordable housing organizations goes well beyond this list, often discouraging even nonprofit developers who might otherwise be inclined to build more affordable housing.

Without understanding how layered and difficult it is to produce, site, maintain and preserve affordable housing, many people find it hard to answer our call-to-action. They don't understand why we don't just build more housing!

So, a great way to use your data is to help people see what is largely invisible to them. Help them see the layered "to-do" list and understand how their support for the solutions we are bringing forward could help us do this work.

This example provides people with a way to breakdown the costs of affordable housing and to know where the levers of change in the existing systems are likely to be. Or at least to understand where the cost drivers are.

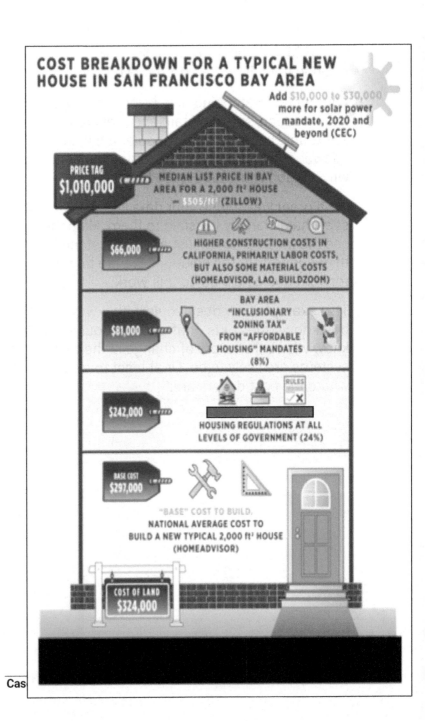

COST BREAKDOWN FOR A TYPICAL NEW HOUSE IN SAN FRANCISCO BAY AREA

Add $10,000 to $30,000 more for solar power mandate, 2020 and beyond (CEC)

PRICE TAG $1,010,000 — MEDIAN LIST PRICE IN BAY AREA FOR A 2,000 ft² HOUSE = $505/ft² (ZILLOW)

$66,000 — HIGHER CONSTRUCTION COSTS IN CALIFORNIA, PRIMARILY LABOR COSTS, BUT ALSO SOME MATERIAL COSTS (HOMEADVISOR, LAO, BUILDZOOM)

$81,000 — BAY AREA "INCLUSIONARY ZONING TAX" FROM "AFFORDABLE HOUSING" MANDATES (8%)

$242,000 — HOUSING REGULATIONS AT ALL LEVELS OF GOVERNMENT (24%)

BASE COST $297,000 — "BASE" COST TO BUILD, NATIONAL AVERAGE COST TO BUILD A NEW TYPICAL 2,000 ft² HOUSE (HOMEADVISOR)

COST OF LAND $324,000

Cas

Use Your Data to Anchor and Credential Concrete Solutions Within those Systems, Not Problems. Rather than start with a set of data describing the problem in detail, start instead with data that helps people focus on the solutions you propose. This means looking for (or collecting) data on the solution. How much of an investment will we need before we see the benefits? How does this solution offset other costs? How many people can this solution help? How much capacity do we need to implement the solution? How long does that solution last, etc.?

Here's an example: Health advocates working to reduce deaths from cardiac arrest could easily run a headline that heralded the number of people who die in our country from cardiac arrest. A more positively framed headline would start with the solution and ask how many more lives could be saved.

How many more people might share another birthday with their loved ones because bystanders knew how to give CPR.

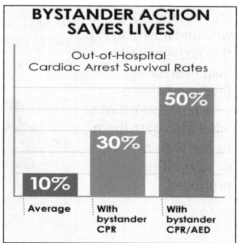

BYSTANDER ACTION SAVES LIVES

Out-of-Hospital Cardiac Arrest Survival Rates

	50%
30%	
10%	
Average	With bystander CPR	With bystander CPR/AED

Here's an example: Health advocates working to reduce childhood obesity, for example, might anchor a systems-level solution by pointing to the number of new parks or open spaces that would need to be created or rehabilitated to provide children with an outlet for physical activity, rather than starting with the number of obese adolescents in a community.

They could share data on how the addition of just 20 parks across "green deserts" in a city, would likely reduce or "flatten the curve" on obesity rates in those communities. They could also highlight what positive things happen for children, their families, and the surrounding community when we flatten the childhood obesity curve.

With respect to the latter, when people have a fuller understanding of why and how solving this issue would help everybody (including these young people), that's what also gets them to see their stake in which you've proposed.

81% of U.S. teachers say kids' behavior changes positively after recess.

Take the chart below, we don't have data or stats on childhood obesity, but we sure do have lots of information about the impacts of play.

Data on where there are "hot spots" of obesity developing across the region could be provided to share the rationale for locating parks in those areas of the city. And, the magnitude of the obesity challenge overall (the problem advocates want to solve) can be embedded later in the case.

The point here though is that by focusing on a defined solutions and giving that the best of our attention in terms of data, we've actually made a stronger case about the need for better parks and playgrounds for children. And if our solutions win the day, we're likely to see fewer children in those neighborhoods struggling with obesity and obesity related chronic diseases.

Here are some other great examples of how we might anchor people in solutions, rather than in problems.

Playrounds are designed to
PULL KIDS AWAY FROM THE SCREEN
and get them excited about outdoor playtime.

We think every child in every community deserves access to **FUN, STIMULATING PLAYGROUNDS.**

DURING PLAY, CHILDREN USE THEIR IMAGINATION as they create fantasy worlds, act out different roles and express their emotions.

Let's take the example of childhood obesity one step further. We could also include data on other systems-level solutions like beverage manufacturers and restaurants. Focusing on what kids eat and who produces what they eat, can draw the conversation back to systems. This kind of data is extremely helpful. It reminds people of the systems issues that can help us tackle this issue at greater scale.

Be clear that this kind of data doesn't absolve parents, caregivers and others of taking responsibility for the children in their care, but it does anchor the solutions at a higher level so that there is balance in the conversations around this issue.

If you don't anchor them in systems, the default to blaming parents for their children's obesity happens without any serious grappling with the broader issues that make it very difficult (even for very conscious parents and caregivers) to respond appropriately.

Use Your Data to Anchor and Inspire the Possibility of Change. Given the current state of most social issues in this country, people are generally very cynical about the possibility that things can really change and be made better. And this is especially true when negative disruptors barge into the conversation. So, there are times when we can leverage our data (and the way that it is framed) to broaden the public imagination – to get them to think beyond the contours of what they already have as a mental reference point.

To help expand people's sense of possibility and raise their optimism about the prospects for change, use your data to give examples of how we might solve the problem – even out-of-the-box examples help. Give examples of how we've solved similar issues like this one in the past or how other industries, organizations, agencies, or residents, were able to triumph over similar challenges.

Here's an example: Several years ago, the Institute of Medicine (IOM) of the National Academies made a set of recommendations to address critical inefficiencies in our health care system. They created a series of info graphics to help stakeholders in the health care system see how similar issues are handled in other sectors.

The IOM could have simply highlighted the costly inefficiencies in the health care delivery system because those systems are not using data effectively or serving patients well or any number of additional issues. Those would have been problem-centric, negatively framed data.

Instead, they chose to highlight how the same kind of information (even sensitive information) is shared in other industries. Their point was to highlight the possibilities for change in the health care system and to inspire action.

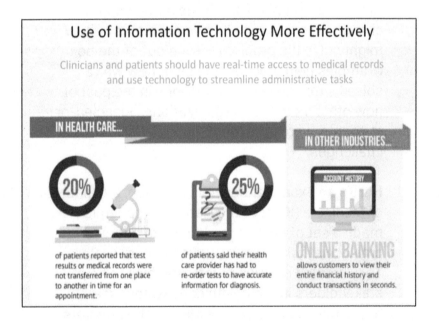

Use of Information Technology More Effectively

Clinicians and patients should have real-time access to medical records and use technology to streamline administrative tasks

IN HEALTH CARE...

IN OTHER INDUSTRIES...

20%

25%

ACCOUNT HISTORY

of patients reported that test results or medical records were not transferred from one place to another in time for an appointment.

of patients said their health care provider has had to re-order tests to have accurate information for diagnosis.

ONLINE BANKING
allows customers to view their entire financial history and conduct transactions in seconds.

In this first infographic, they show how health care institutions make use of the same (or similar) technologies as banks currently use. Banks too have highly sensitive information, but they use that data to make their processes much more efficient and better service the needs of their customers. IOM positions these two sectors side-by-side in the infographic to make the similarities visually meaningful and to drive home the larger point – we could be so much more effective in serving our patients if we made some systems-level changes.

There are a couple additional examples from IOM on the same theme – comparing how health care systems handle and learn from the data they collect versus the experience in other sectors.

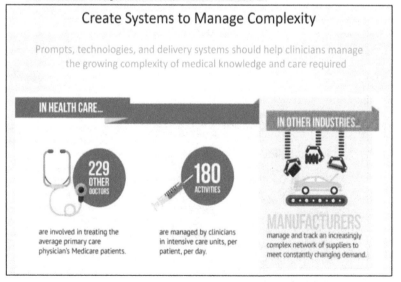

Create Systems to Manage Complexity

Prompts, technologies, and delivery systems should help clinicians manage the growing complexity of medical knowledge and care required

IN HEALTH CARE...

IN OTHER INDUSTRIES...

229 OTHER DOCTORS

180 ACTIVITIES

MANUFACTURERS

are involved in treating the average primary care physician's Medicare patients.

are managed by clinicians in intensive care units, per patient, per day.

manage and track an increasingly complex network of suppliers to meet constantly changing demand.

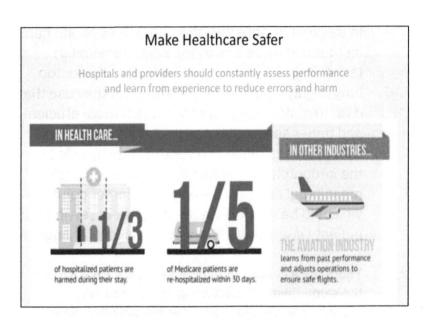

Make Healthcare Safer

Hospitals and providers should constantly assess performance and learn from experience to reduce errors and harm

IN HEALTH CARE...

IN OTHER INDUSTRIES...

1/3
of hospitalized patients are harmed during their stay.

1/5
of Medicare patients are re-hospitalized within 30 days.

THE AVIATION INDUSTRY
learns from past performance and adjusts operations to ensure safe flights.

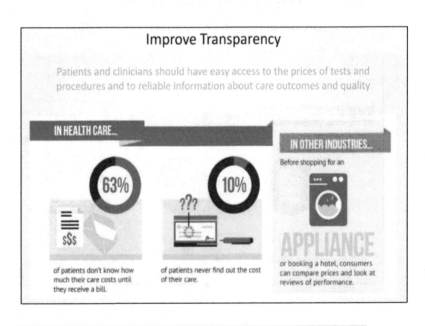

Improve Transparency

Patients and clinicians should have easy access to the prices of tests and procedures and to reliable information about care outcomes and quality

IN HEALTH CARE...

IN OTHER INDUSTRIES...

Before shopping for an

63%
of patients don't know how much their care costs until they receive a bill.

10%

???
of patients never find out the cost of their care.

APPLIANCE
or booking a hotel, consumers can compare prices and look at reviews of performance.

Use Your Data to Create "Social Math" to Improve People's Understanding of Your Solutions, Anchor Them, and Inspire the Possibility of Change.
Social math is a technique used to help people understand the logic and magnitude of the data you are providing. When done well, social math allows you to make deeper meaning for people. In casemaking, social math is essential. Most people have a hard time processing and really digesting all of the data that is thrown at them (usually without context), so social math helps people makes sense of what we're trying to convey with our data. The idea here is to use social math to help people relate the data you have about your solutions to something they can easily relate to. Mastering the fine art of helping people make sense of your data by relating it to what they already know, is a great way to leverage your data for stronger casemaking.

Here's an example: One of the most challenging aspects of trying to get people excited about the solutions we have to homelessness is that most people believe the costs to do so are unrealistic. They size up the problem (mentally, in their heads) and then often think, *we can't possibly solve that issue, it's too big and the cost would be too great.* Once they've made that mental assessment, it's harder to mobilize them to action on this issue.

Social math can help. An article that ran in the Huffington post with the caption "U.S. Could End Homelessness with Money Used to Buy Christmas Decorations" is an example.

The beauty of the example is that it puts the cost of ending homelessness in perspective. It actually isn't out of the realm of possibility that we could end homelessness (at least in terms of its costs).

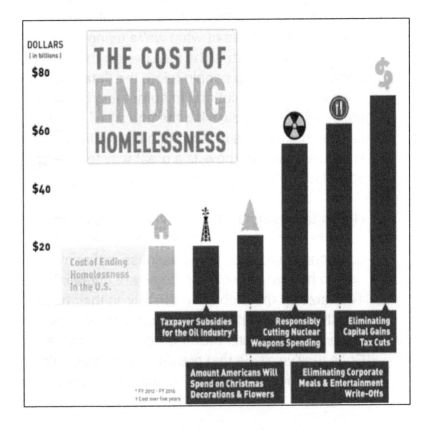

By sacrificing even the smallest of things (the cost of new holiday decorations), we could actually achieve something pretty phenomenal. Be clear, the graphic is not asking people to ACTUALLY stop buying holiday decorations, it only asks us to entertain the idea that with a few adjustments in how we spend, we could end a crisis that is heartbreaking to watch unfold across our nation.

This social math helps people connect a big issue (homelessness) with the possibility of change. Think about other kinds of costs that we could easily compare to something most people take for granted. To do so excites people's sense of what is possible and makes the large problem seem conquerable.

And to reiterate and be clear – the point here is not to really ask people to stop purchasing their holiday decorations. To the contrary, our point is to make people reconsider what is possible and give them the space to ask questions about the possibility of other solutions. Social math for casemaking can be effectively created in a variety of ways. The approach above (homelessness intervention related to holiday decorations) is the first approach. It means taking the data you have and comparing it (in scale and number) to something that is more easily understandable to your stakeholders.

Here's another social math example: Many advocates in the environmental space have extolled the virtues of solar power and other forms of clean energy but we are still so fossil fuel dependent. One way to help people understand the power and potential of alternatives, is to compare the tradeoffs between what we could generate with solar power versus what we do today using fossil fuels. By using our data to lay out the possibilities, we excite people's imagination about what could be done and give them a way to think about the possibilities of changing course.

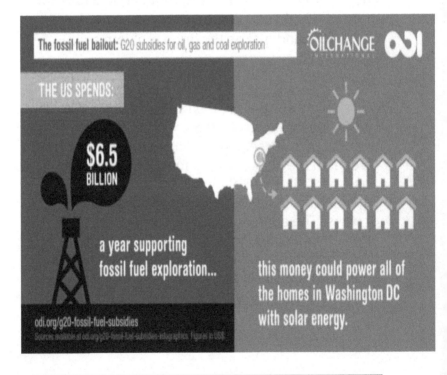

The fossil fuel bailout: G20 subsidies for oil, gas and coal exploration

OILCHANGE ODI

THE US SPENDS:

$6.5 BILLION

a year supporting fossil fuel exploration...

this money could power all of the homes in Washington DC with solar energy.

odi.org/g20-fossil-fuel-subsidies

Here's another social math example: The alcohol industry spends more than $2 billion every year to advertise and promote consumption by college students. This amounts to approximately $225,000 every hour of every day.

The result? Instead of just giving the numbers – do it using social math. Say this instead:

- *Enough alcohol was consumed by college students last year to fill 30,000 Olympic-size swimming pools.*
- *The overall amount spent on alcohol per student exceeded the dollars spent on books and was far greater than the combined amount of all fellowships and scholarships provided to students in the United States.*

Then develop visuals to help people see the numbers provided, like the infographic below.

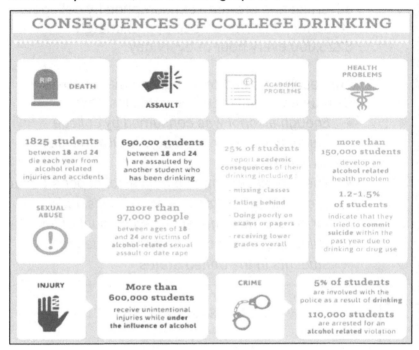

And although not everybody thinks the consumption of alcohol as a social investment, it is! When you add up all the dollars spent and the impact it has on our young people, it is absolutely a social investment that might be better used differently – if we could make the case! So, as we evaluate this data, we could ask ourselves if our societal investment in alcohol is a useful one and how we might help our young people make better and more lasting investments in their (and our) future.

To push this even further, we might highlight the broader social and economic consequences of these investments and use our data to do so. In the example here, we can see that alcohol interlock installation in all vehicles would almost solve the problem of alcohol related fatalities in our country.

Prevention Impact of Mandatory Alcohol Ignition Lock

<u>Over 15 years, alcohol interlock installation in all new US vehicles would result in:</u>

85% of alcohol-involved crash fatalities prevented (> 59,000)

84-88% of nonfatal alcohol-involved crash injuries prevented (> 1.25 million)

$342 Billion in injury-related costs saved

- *Greatest benefit among recently legal drinking drivers*
- *Cost savings outweighed installation costs after 3 years*

Alcohol interlock installation in all new vehicles is a cost-effective prevention policy that can substantially reduce alcohol-involved crash fatalities and injuries.

Another variation uses social math to break numbers down, making the problem smaller and more easily solved. This is important because some of the most profound social issues feel too big to be solved. We can use our data to bring the problem down to a level that people can start to imagine how it might be solved. Let's continue with the alcohol consumption example.

Here's another social math example: One of the most common ways of using social math is to highlight the impact of an issue but break it down into smaller numbers so that people can absorb its importance is to look at time and money.

On this issue of alcohol consumption, we might ask a different question, what's the incidence of the issue over a period (as in the example below) and how much does it cost ALL OF US in dollars (an annual amount)? Again, the importance here is that people can relate to these smaller numbers and to the concern with costs.

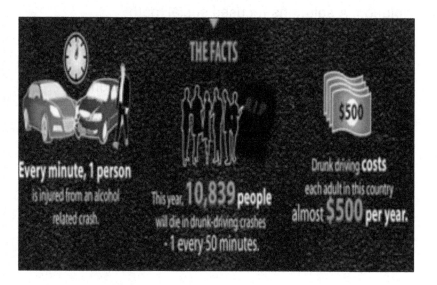

Here's another social math example: This time we apply social math to prescription drug use. Here, the larger number of painkillers is reduced to the day, per capita. By using the data in this way, advocates make this something that more people are likely to be able to digest and understand. If this infographic were also paired with a solutions-based one, it would promote both understanding of the magnitude of the problem and its potential solution. A solutions-focused social math infographic on this might focus on how often doctor's prescribed holistic medicine to address pain and helped patients avoid the likely side-effects of painkillers. Those infographics might also estimate the decrease in addiction because medical professionals gave patients options that did not cause dependency on synthetic drugs.

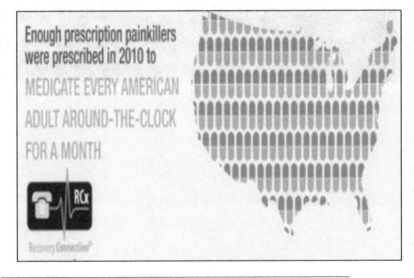

Enough prescription painkillers were prescribed in 2010 to MEDICATE EVERY AMERICAN ADULT AROUND-THE-CLOCK FOR A MONTH

Recovery Connection®

Use Your Data to Anchor People In the Kinds of Comparisons Between Policy Approaches that Help Make Your Solutions Seem More Feasible. Yet another way to leverage your data for stronger casemaking is to highlight how our existing policy choices are inconsistent with the values we hold and are not serving us well in terms of the impacts they engender.

Here's an example: Because policy is made at all levels of government and in different agencies, it is not uncommon to see one branch of government or agency promoting an outcome that another branch or agency is discouraging. Highlighting this disconnect is a good use of our data, because it helps people conclude that we need to change course – choosing a more thoughtful and consistent policy direction.

Our example here comes from the education space. Head Start (something we are currently defunding at a rapid pace) has been shown to have a larger effect on children's early achievement than giving homework (for older children). So, if we're looking for opportunities to advance educational achievement, the investments made early on (as early as pre-kindergarten) have a bigger effect than we see when we give children homework, in later years of their educational trajectory.

No, this doesn't mean we shouldn't give homework, it just means we should take another look at Head Start. If Head Start is working to great effect (and working better than our other education programs), why defund it?

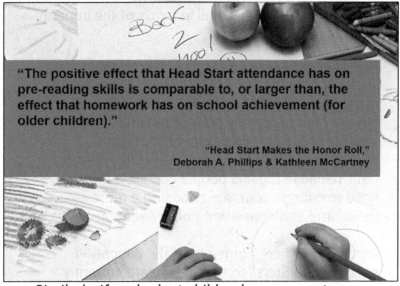

"The positive effect that Head Start attendance has on pre-reading skills is comparable to, or larger than, the effect that homework has on school achievement (for older children)."

"Head Start Makes the Honor Roll,"
Deborah A. Phillips & Kathleen McCartney

Similarly, if we look at children's exposure to violent media, we could make a similar argument. In the next example, the author highlights the relationship between violent media (video games, television programing, etc.) and aggression (especially in children). The fact that violent media (something we don't really regulate) acts as a more powerful stimuli for children's behavior than many of the things we do regulate, says our policy efforts may be misplaced.

There is a case to be made for regulating violent media in spaces where children are present and our action in other areas of children's development, speaks volumes for us. Why haven't we focused more policy attention regulating (or at least addressing) the clear impact of violent media as well? These data suggest that we should!

"The correlation between violent media and aggression is larger than the effect that wearing a condom has on decreasing the risk of HIV,...larger than the correlation between exposure to lead and decreased IQ levels in kids,...larger than the effects of exposure to asbestos, larger than the effect of secondhand smoke on cancer."

Brad Bushman,
Professor of Psychology, Iowa State University

Use Your Data to Anchor People's Thinking in the Benefits of Our Collective Intervention at the Program, Policy or Investment Level. It goes without saying that the primary reason that we are using data as part of our casemaking is that we want to mobilize people in support of solutions that can help. It's interesting however that most of us use our data to credential the problem, but not to credential the interventions (our intended destination). People need more information and data on the intervention that you propose than on the problem itself. They need to know how it works, who it would help most, limitations or drawbacks, as well as the benefits that would accrue to everybody because you are intervening in this way). So, use your data to help meet that need - credential the intervention.

Here's an example: If we continue with the alcohol consumption example from earlier, we could gather data on how a wide variety of community actors, institutions, agencies, or residents are ready and able to directly intervene. Here's an example that focuses on health care providers and it's a great use of data anchoring. This anchors people in the kind of intervention that might be most helpful.

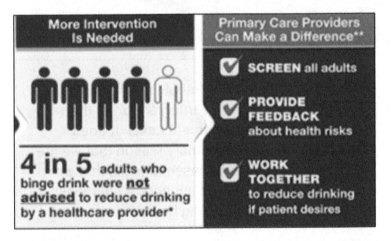

It reminds us that there are clear intervention points (largely medical professionals) and how we might take advantage of those points.

Here's another useful example: This graph focused on the COVID-19 virus has been shared widely and helped many Americans understand the severity of the issue and importance of 'social distancing' as an immediate intervention. Not everyone complied with all of the COVID-19 interventions (masking and vaccines were particularly controversial) but most Americans were convinced enough to follow general precautions and graphs like this one helped get them there.

The graph shows the impact of taking protective measures (like masking, social distancing, etc.) and the difference it would make above and beyond what our health care system could do alone. In this way, it made the point that without our collective and intentional work to help, our health care systems would be ineffectual at solving this issue. In other words, the action here was about ordinary people helping to produce better outcomes.

Most notably, by showing the limitations of our formal channels of health (the dotted line across the middle), people were able to see the importance of their behavior changes for all of us. Again, not everybody was convinced by this kind of information, but keep in mind that most Americans actually did take precautionary measures that helped to slow the spread of COVID-19, to everyone's benefit. Think how many other ways we might share data to help people see their efficacy in shifting how they show up in community.

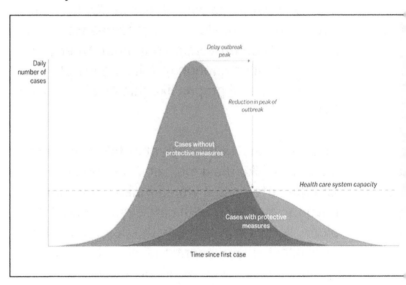

Use Your Data to Anchor People's Thinking in the Intersectional Nature of the Challenges We Face (Highlighting the Connections That Most People Don't Have Much Practice Thinking About). Remember that most of the challenges we face in our nation today are not technical challenges, they are adaptive challenges. That means they are challenges that know no boundaries and are unlikely to be solved by one sector, one group, or one industry. Adaptive problems require collective effort from many people in our communities to solve and often, they require us to think more holistically about solutions.

Yet, many of our organizations are not practiced in thinking holistically about the challenges we face, for a variety of reasons. Sometimes funding for our organizations or agencies are siloed, sometimes our focus is siloed, and sometimes, it is just easier to just work within our sphere of influence, so we do...to the detriment of true holistic solutions.

Data can help us move people to more holistic, cross-sector thinking and action, if we use them for this purpose. Whenever possible, use your data to highlight the connections between sectors, issue-areas, or communities to anchor people's ability to think more holistically about the issues at the heart of your case.

Here's an example: Most doctors will tell you that many of the real-world challenges that people face show up in their offices. People's stress at work or in their personal relationships, for example, show up in their blood pressure or ulcers. Living in a food desert can show up as diabetes because people in a community may be overconsuming processed, fatty, and sugary food. In other words, we know that the social environments in which people exist show up in the reality of our health status.

In this example, physicians were surveyed about how they diagnose and treat patients for things happening in their social environments. An overwhelming majority of physicians said that they would love to write prescriptions for the broader social issues that are making their patients sick – lack of affordable housing, jobs, nutritional assistance, healthy food programs, etc. However, they don't have the ability to write those prescriptions for the cause of their patients' illnesses.

The survey of physicians discussed in the infographic, found that physicians overwhelmingly believed that addressing the underlying causes (and even just asking patients about their lives), would dramatically improve patient care and outcomes.

Moreover, 3 out of 4 physicians surveyed said they wished health insurers would pay for the additional costs associated with connecting their patients with relevant services, since it would take them additional time and money to assess these additional needs and make referrals or recommendations to community partners. Who better to assess and refer people, struggling with physical health needs, than their doctors?

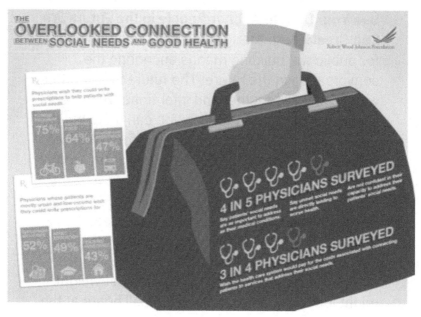

We might also produce a similar graphic for teachers and police officers. Many of them see the impacts of the social environments around people but are not empowered with the resources to address those issues impacting their lives or outcomes. However, our ability to show the connections between these institutions to the

challenges that people are facing in other areas of their lives, gives us the opportunity to
see people are whole – requiring solutions that require a holistic, intersectional lens.

Use Your Data to Anchor People in the Future We Can Create Together. Additionally, leveraging data for public will building means anchoring the conversation in the future! The future is something we can create together and intentionally. So, one of the most important things you can do to build support for your systems-change effort is ensure that it has a strong future orientation at the front end.

People tend to romanticize past successes, recalling their own personal sacrifice more than the systems that supported them. For example, someone who worked very hard and lost weight might look back years later and recall hours at the gym and snacking on carrot sticks but not acknowledge the new bike lanes that encouraged biking to work or the healthy food markets that opened nearby. As a result, when people look backward, their willingness to support larger interventions like bike lanes and healthy good markets, are not likely to be robust. That's where our data comes in!
Invite your stakeholders to imagine the future they can help create and use your data to

reinforce that orientation.

Here's an example: This example comes from the animal shelter field. Often relegated to providing care and protection for animals in need, one such shelter decided to set a much higher and fundamental intention. By 2030 their goal is to end animal abandonment in their city. By showing the ladder needed to get there and the impact that they could have, they made this larger, very ambitious goal feel much more tangible.

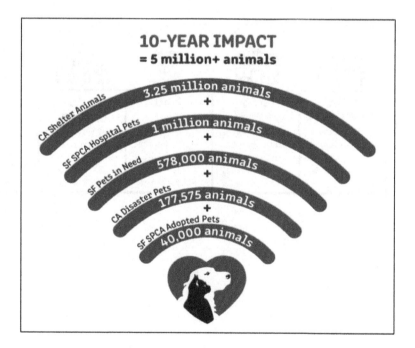

Here's another relevant example: This example of using data to enhance a future orientation is to underscore the impact that you expect in the future due to the investment that you are asking your stakeholders and strategic partners to make. That helps them to see the outcomes that you are after (and expect to have), as well as to keep the conversation forward facing. This is an example of how people can be made to see their investment in the future state of our community.

Invest in a life today! Just look at what your monthly gift can impact:

$100	$75	$50	$35	$20
or $3.30 a day	or $2.50 a day	or $1.65 a day	or $1.15 a day	or 65 cents a day
monthly provides highly specialized case management services to at-risk families and youth	monthly provides sustainability for daily upkeep of our programs, services and facility	monthly provides an individual with one night of shelter and security including 2 meals	monthly provides 1 hour of case management and linkage to services in the community	monthly supports transportation for 5 people to jobs, interviews, medical needs and more

Here's an example: If we look at the issue of homelessness, we find another example of using our data to advance a future orientation. In the infographic below, the idea is to anchor public thinking in prevention and how that prevention flattens the incidence of homelessness.

This kind of use of data is especially important on issues like homelessness where public spending in some communities has increased to solve this issue but due to a variety of factors, homelessness has remained an issue. The future orientation in this data chart gets people focused on the long-term outcome and gives them concrete data on what prevention today, means for our tomorrow. We need to remind people that our intentional efforts today will have future outcomes that we all want.

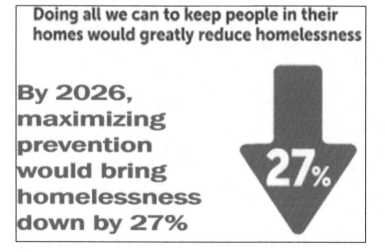

Doing all we can to keep people in their homes would greatly reduce homelessness

By 2026, maximizing prevention would bring homelessness down by 27%

27%

Use Your Data to Anchor People on the ROI AND the SROI of Your Solutions. One of the absolute best uses of our data for casemaking is to give more specificity to our conversation about the investment we need to make in our future. When we talk about the future and its possibility, people can certainly get excited but when we pair that proposition with concrete numbers on the return-on-investment (ROI) and the social return on investment (SROI), we are able to give even more credibility to our solutions.

An ROI might simply mean, do we get a financial return on the investment that we are making in a specific intervention or solution. So, for example, a jobs training program that costs our city $15 million to start might deliver $100 million in return, as the trainees receive less from public assistance and more from earned income (resulting in higher tax revenues). The same jobs program might also produce fantastic social returns as well, since trainees might also find themselves more motivated, healthier, productively employed, etc. In addition, they might make more use of public transportation (driving up revenues there as well). So, our ability to show the ROI and SROI with our data, can go a long way toward making the case for specific interventions or solutions.

Here's an example: The data used to support affordable housing programs, services and investments is often lodged at the individual families and the financial benefits of them having affordable housing. Those are important benefits to share but they pail in comparison to the larger benefits to all of us because these programs, services, and investments are being made. In fact, we know that most of these interventions have benefits that go far beyond their direct beneficiaries and beyond housing. In the chart below we see an example of a housing organization being explicit about how their investment in affordable housing actually translates in other residual (but equally important) benefits like reduced stress, increased school attendance for kids, better performance in school for those kids and in the long-term, stronger economic stability for the kids when they are adults. The ROI might be calculated with data about the housing stability but the latter parts of this chart really get to the SROI. Data exists that can estimate the size of the effect at each phase of the result outlined here.

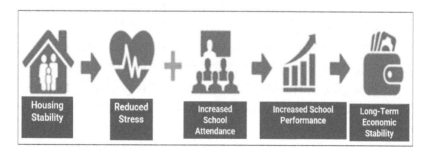

Here's an example: The example below is focused on health care and shows the ROI for health care institutions as they think through options to invest in (and improve) employee health.

Use Your Data to Anchor People's Thinking In the Current Allocation of Resources and How Those Resources Might be Differently Invested to Greater Impact. For many casemakers, the issue of how resources are spent – either by government or by corporate entities – is a major issue. Resource allocation is an important role that governments often control or regulate but it can be difficult to get people to focus attention here. Data highlighting misaligned resource allocations (intentionally or those misalignments out of natural consumption patterns) are important to highlight and share with your stakeholders.

Using your data to highlight how resources are allocated and the impact of those misaligned allocations, can be a great way to leverage your data in the service of public will building. Use that data to prompt a series of questions about how we could re-align those resources (or regulate them when they show up as part of natural consumption), to better effect. Our earlier example of college students' consumption of alcohol and how it outstrips the money they spend on books and tuition, is one example. See a couple others outlined below.

Here's an example: For many years, health advocates have discussed how misaligned the resources in our health care systems are. That is, our dollars are spent in ways that are not serving the highest needs and as a result, our health care system struggles to be as impactful as it could be.

Look at the next chart that outlines how resources for wellness are spent in the United States. The infographic shows that as consumers we spend trillions of dollars on band-aid solutions to things that might be better solved with other interventions, solutions or choices it the marketplace. In the United States we spend substantially more (2x) on personal beauty aids (likely a result of the billions in beauty marketing by corporate retailers), as we do on preventative and public health.

GLOBAL WELLNESS ECONOMY:
$4.5 Trillion Market

Yes, we all want to look our best deep into our elder years (and hence, the focus on anti-aging aids) but when we put those numbers side-by-side, most people would say that their preference would be to shift those resources to public health and preventative care for the growing chronic diseases that today plague our communities.

Each year for example more than 650,000 Americans end up in medical bankruptcy and medical expenses result in more than 60% of all bankruptcies in the United States.

This data might help many people see that the way in which we are spending (and thereby, allocating our health care dollars) may not be the best opportunities to preserve our health. Helping people understand the importance of saving for late-stage illnesses not covered by health care insurers, is critical. Or, helping people see that a nationalized health care system would help millions of Americans avoid bankruptcy courts, is a great use of our data.

Let's state here again, it may not be possible to shift consumption patterns for beauty and anti-aging products (something the beauty industry would likely counter) but making that comparison opens up the possibility for thinking more expansively about the kind of shifts we need to reallocate resources to address bigger, more systemic issues.

Here's an example: Lobbying data gives us another example. This infographic highlights how lobbying has a huge ROI but likely has opportunity costs for other kinds of investments that could be served by the investment in lobbying. In particular, the amount of money spent in the United States on lobbying, if spent differently, could solve a great many problems we face as a nation. So instead of giving some groups, organizations, and industries the advantage of access to power (which is what lobbying is), we could use these funds to greater effect. So anti-lobbying changes or taking the power out of the hands of legislators for a variety of things that do not require their input, could make a world of difference. The graph below might help us use our data to make that case.

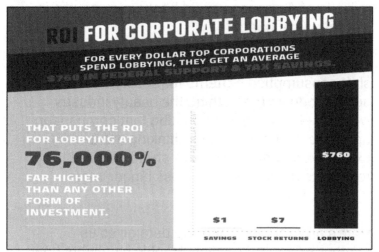

Use Your Data to Anchor, Redirect, or Pivot the Conversation Back to Your Narrative. In Principle #4 on dominant narratives, we focused some intentional practice on the art of an effective pivot. The data you choose and how you wield that data can help you make an effective pivot away from issues that are not helpful and back to the narrative that builds support for your case. During the process of a pivot, data can be used effectively to redirect the conversation back to the anchors that are more meaningful and constructive to your stakeholder.

Here's an example: Here there are two examples that when taken together, help us see a data pivot. In the first picture below, a member of the U.S. House of Representatives is making the case that we don't need nationalized health care because our consumption patterns (if altered) would give us money to pay for health care.

"Americans have choices, and they've got to make a choice. So rather than getting that new iPhone that they just love and want to go spend hundreds of dollars on that, maybe they should invest in their own health care. They've got to make those decisions themselves."

-- Rep. Jason Chaffetz during a CNN interview March 7, 2017

The pivot back: Get back to the narrative the health care advocates want to have about health care costs.

In the second picture, we could use our data as part of an effective pivot back to a narrative that works in our favor. What's important to note here (as stated in the discussion of an effective pivot), is that this is NOT about refuting the argument directly. Sharing this data simply allows you the space to pivot back to a narrative that is more helpful.

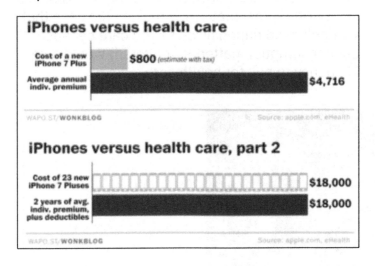

So, you might say something like this.

Yes, I'd love to talk about the cost of iPhones. Let me pull mine out! A brand-new iPhone or some other variety might cost someone $800. But that's not nearly what a health care premium costs workers in almost ANY occupation in the United States today.

So, let's talk about what health care premiums cost workers and who can afford to pay that. The data I share below puts those costs in better perspective. And if you'd like, we could even call each other on our iPhones to talk about that!"

That effectively redirects the conversation back to data that helps you to have the conversation YOU want to have and that is more meaningful to the issue at hand.

$16,655
Average annual premium per enrolled employee for a family on employer-based health insurance.

$5,832
Average single annual premium per enrolled employee for employer-based health insurance.

Less than $1,200
It's estimated 8 in 10 individuals can choose a Marketplace plan with a premium of $100 or less per month after tax credits.

That's a pivot using your data in support of a bigger narrative shift. We might even share more data about the cost of a healthy care premium to further shift the conversation back to how we allocate resources to what matters.

Lastly, we could even use good social math to help people see the allocation of resources in health care and ask people to think with us about how we might produce policies that help us get to a more thoughtful allocation.

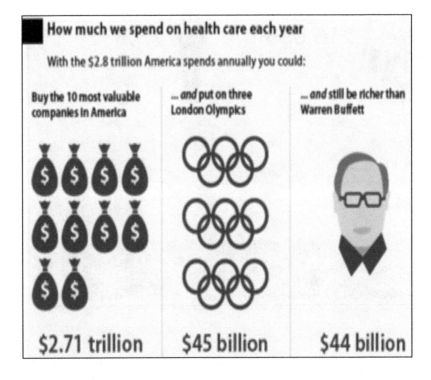

How much we spend on health care each year

With the $2.8 trillion America spends annually you could:

Buy the 10 most valuable companies in America

...and put on three London Olympics

...and still be richer than Warren Buffett

$2.71 trillion

$45 billion

$44 billion

The Only Time It is Helpful to Anchor Your Case with Negatively Framed Data is When You Have A New Piece of Data that is Startling or Shocking. Use that <u>One Data Point</u> and Then Pivot Back to Data That Helps Highlight Your Solutions. The recommendation is to avoid negatively framed data at the top of your casemaking. However, that doesn't mean you cannot use such data, it just means DON'T LEAD with that negative data. There is however one circumstance where leading with negatively framed data can be to your advantage. If you have one dramatic data point that is new – meaning, it is not something that people familiar with the issue know about. Using that data in your case can be helpful because it "slow brains" the issue. That is, it opens the case with something unusual that can grab people's attention in a new way, slows them down, and forces their brains to grapple with this new information. (Note, we talk more about slow braining in Principle 7 on storytelling).

<u>Here's the caveat, you only need to use ONE data point negatively framed</u> and then pivot quickly back to your solutions. In other words, use the data as the flash point in the conversation but quickly get back to the stronger ground of the opportunities in front of us to tackle the issue.

Here's an example: In most of the world, children cannot be sentenced to death or life-sentences in jails. The United States is one of the few places in the world where this is the case. Highlighting how rare it is that nations engage in this practice and the impacts on their families, can be a game-changer for child justice advocates.

Here we remind people that although we like to think of ourselves as more advanced and humane on issues of human rights, on the issue of child justice we are one of the worst. So this data point, negatively framed, forces us to grapple with whether we have been humane on this issue.

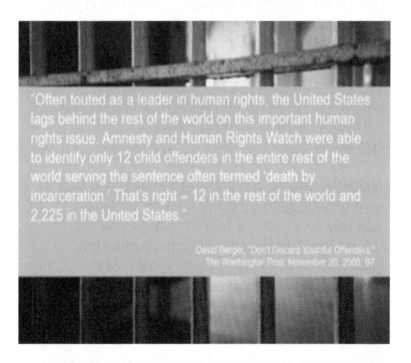

"Often touted as a leader in human rights, the United States lags behind the rest of the world on this important human rights issue. Amnesty and Human Rights Watch were able to identify only 12 child offenders in the entire rest of the world serving the sentence often termed 'death by incarceration.' That's right – 12 in the rest of the world and 2,225 in the United States."

David Berger, "Don't Discard Youthful Offenders," The Washington Post, November 20, 2005, B7

A Final Word: Be Careful Not to Use Labels in Your Data that Stigmatize Certain Groups or Use Data in Ways that Can Lead to "Othering". Negatively framed data is problematic for many reasons, one of the most important is that you can inadvertently contribute to stigmatization or reinforcing stereotypes or bias. Rethink how you label the groups in your charts – labels like "at-risk", "vulnerable", "homeless people" or "under-privileged" – all stand the risk of reinforcing very unproductive negative biases and stigma. You can make the same points with your data to distinguish groups without negatively labeling people. Actually, think about what would happen if you labeled people in terms of their potential for greatness, rather than their vulnerabilities?

Here's an example: Many organizations working with people who are experiencing homelessness, simply label them as "homeless people". But homelessness is not a characteristic of innate abilities, it is a condition or experience that people are facing. So, let's call it what it actually is. This example takes a statistic that is normally presented in the negative case and with the negative label (i.e. the number of "homeless people" who die every day).

Through the Investment We Are Making in Our Community, We Will Save the

36

people who are experiencing homelessness

would die on the street today, without our help.

and

Here, we show this in a different way – how many of our neighbors could be spared the debilitating experience of homelessness, if we changed how we allocate resources or invested differently in our housing priorities?

To Avoid "Othering", When Possible and Appropriate, Use Your Data to Present the Universality of Problems, Even When Your Policy Solutions Target Specific Groups or Sub-Populations (i.e. Often for the Benefit of Equity Concerns). It is very easy for people who are experiencing poverty or other challenging circumstances to be labeled or "othered" because of our data. One way to avoid that is to demonstrate the universality of the problem (where appropriate) and then let your narrative speak to the reasons why you have chosen to focus on particular groups or populations.

Here's an example: Almost all Americans are experiencing increases in their housing costs relative to their incomes. Yet, most housing organizations single out low-income families and talk a lot about the fact that many of them are "housing cost burdened" – meaning, they pay more than 30% of their income for housing. By framing it this way, they can easily be "othered" by people who will say "those people" simply lack the ability to manage their finances properly.

While it may be true that people could be educated in ways that help them manage their finances better (couldn't we all?), that is not the primary reason so many Americans are struggling to afford a decent place to live. Instead of talking solely about the plight of people who earn low wages, show the universality of what is happening and THEN, explain the rationale for focusing policy on those groups.

Here is an example showing that people at all income levels were paying more of their income for housing in 2014 (the blue bars) versus 2005 (the red bars). So, this is an experience that is happening to EVERYONE, not simply to people earning low wages.

This kind of representation makes it difficult to suggest that workers with low wages are somehow less capable of managing their finances than others. We might however argue (as many housing advocates do) that people earning lower wages may have to make tougher tradeoffs to pay rent than others and so, our focus on those workers is warranted.

Cost Burdened (30% or more)

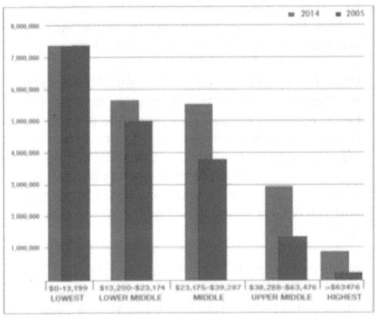

Here's an example: Another example uses social math to show how economic inequality is growing across all income groups (relative to others) but how it is widening more in lower income bands. This is not new data but typically it is shared by advocates saying something like this: The bottom 20% of US family incomes grew by only 6% between 1979 and 2008. This is a major decline when compared to income growth between 1947 and 1979.

Instead, this infographic highlights how all groups (except the top income earners) are faring different outcomes than they did in previous generations. By showing the full spectrum, it makes it more difficult to "other" today's low-wage earners to suggest that they are doing something uniquely wrong that is causing their disadvantaged status.

Comparing the Growth of U.S. Family Incomes

An infographic by United for a Fair Economy

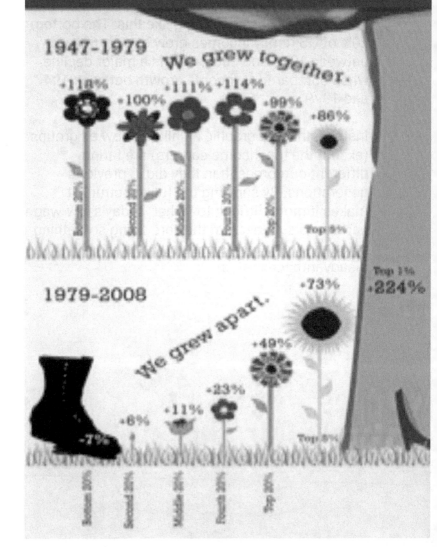

1947-1979 — We grew together.

- +118% Bottom 20%
- +100% Second 20%
- +111% Middle 20%
- +114% Fourth 20%
- +99% Top 20%
- +86% Top 5%

1979-2008 — We grew apart.

- -7% Bottom 20%
- +6% Second 20%
- +11% Middle 20%
- +23% Fourth 20%
- +49% Top 20%
- +73% Top 5%
- +224% Top 1%

Here's an example: Another example shares state-wide data on the incidence of poverty. This graph shows that no matter where you live in the state, there are children whose family incomes are so low that they live deeply in poverty. In other words, this is not a Miami problem or an Orlando or Tallahassee problem. This is an adaptive challenge that is state-wide. The magnitude in each county might be different but the challenge itself is spread across the entire state. This representation makes it difficult for people to create unconstructive narratives othering or stereotyping different parts of the state or the different constellations that live in those parts of the state.

Anchoring and social math are important pro-tips. The opportunities for creative, accurate use of data are considerable, and the value of these pro-tips are great. As you use them, just be sure that your data, stats and comparisons are accurate and defensible.

There are 944,415 children under 18 years old living in Florida. Here is where they live.

Source: 2015 Data from U.S. Census, American Community Survey

INSTEAD OF THIS: After more than a decade of progress in improving high school graduation rates, there remains about 1,300 traditional high schools in need of serious improvement and redesign, according to new research from the GraduateNet campaign. Among them are more than 800 low-graduation-rate high schools with an average graduation rate of 49 percent. From the inner city to the heartland, these high schools sit at the fault lines of race, class and inequity in the US.

TRY THIS: We are winning the battle to improve high School graduation rates – we've already improved learning and graduation rates at 4,500 schools nationwide. Now, let's finish what we started – working to improve and redesign the remaining 1,300 schools with low graduation rates. We will redouble our efforts to provide resources, expertise, counselors and student assistance to the 800 high schools with the lowest graduation rates. And, by 2030, our efforts will ensure that every high school across this nation, no matter where it is located, prepares its students for success and sends them out with an earned degree! By investing in the students who need it most, we will address the equity issues at the

---

center of our educational system and better academic achevement for all students. We can do it, we're already winning. Will you join our effort to do even more?

INSTEAD OF THIS: There are 4,475 children in foster care in our state. It's important to pause in our hectic schedules to remember these statistics:

- 1 child becomes homeless every 14 min
- 1 child drops out of school every 60 min
- 1 child is abused/neglected every 60 min

We know that some of the children in these statistics are our children. They attend our schools, live in our neighborhoods, maybe even have dinner at our tables. They are the reason we do so much to focus on PREVENTION.

TRY THIS: Our future depends on our ability to ensure that the 2+ million children in our state have the resources, resilience, and strong start in life that they need to carry us forward. This is an awesome responsibility that all of us must steward the future of so many children in our state. We've done a lot already to help the children across this state have what they need to thrive and are on the road to success in our great state.

Our work now is to make sure that the 4,475 children who remain in foster care across our state, get the same great start. Have we done enough to ensure that these children have the bright future that we all envision for all our children? Because of our collective effort:

- We find a home for 1 child every 90 min
- We re-enroll a child back in school every 120 min
- We remove a child who is in danger at home and find a safer place for them to live, every 3 hours

We know that with a focus on prevention, it is totally possible for us to help families avoid foster care entirely and ensure that the 4,475 children already in foster care across our state, find stable homes.

Here's why it matters! With our help, some of these children will become nurses – working the front lines in our hospitals or caring for our growing senior population allowing many of them to age-in-place.

Some will become business owners, leading some of our most innovative companies or serve in public office. Some will become police officers – helping to maintain law and order in our communities.

Some will be managers of the retail outlets where we shop – helping us to choose ripe produce or select that perfect suit for our daughter's wedding. Some will become teachers and social workers – helping us to prepare the next generation of children for success.

Our success is riding on our ability to pull ALL of our children forward. No one wins if so many of our children do not have what they need to thrive. No one wins if so many children experience long-term homelessness or if they never learn how to function in stable families into adulthood. No one wins if children across our state have so little to start with, that they become more susceptible to child predators or drug dealers.

We only win when all of our children have what they need to survive: stable homes, adults who surround them in love, and communities who nurture their success.

4,475 brilliant lives are in our hands – join the effort to ensure their light continues to shine in every community across our state. Let's make sure that their experiences with caregivers, get's beter from here. Let's make sure that the future ahead of them, looks better than their pasts. Help us to fight as hard for their futures, as we fight for our own children.

You can join us by:
- **Advocating** on behalf of fostering in our state
- **Contributing** your time and expertise to our foster parents as resources
- **Sponsoring** a "foster day" at your place of worship, school or place of employment
- **Fundraising** to help us close the gap in funding that our agencies get from public dollars.

KEEP
CALM
AND
Use Data
Wisely

Principle #6: Make Inequitable Systems the Villain

Often, I hear leaders talk about the need for "systems change" and most of the time they talk about this kind of change in the context of seeking equity. They want to change the workforce development _system_ or the educational _system_, or our electoral _system_, and much more. These governance systems were designed long ago, before most of us were doing the work that we do today, and most are badly in need a repair, reimagination and redesign. These governance systems simply are not functioning well enough to address the wide range and scale of the challenges we face today, partially because they were built for a different time.

I also know that what motivates the systems focus for most justice seekers and changemakers, is the desire to see more equitable outcomes in our society. Without a real look at how anti-black racism has been deeply embedded in how our governance systems were built and how they function today, we won't be honest about our shared history as part of the case that we're making.

It's no secret that most of our governance

systems were built to protect social privilege. Racism, sexism, ablism, individualism, homophobia and more, were intentionally built into the structure of those governance systems. So much so, that even if we were to remove all the leaders in charge of operating those systems and replace them with more empathetic leaders, we'd likely still realize the same outcomes.

Because inequalities have been built directly into the structure of those systems, we won't get to better and more equitable outcomes without doing the surgical work of going deep to get the root causes. One of the most significant roles of leaders is that they recognize when deeper structural changes are needed, and they understand how those systems can be adapted to better meet our needs. While leaders may understand when an overhaul of an existing system is needed to help it function better, they need broad support from stakeholders (both institutional stakeholders and broader public audiences) to get that done.

And, as many leaders know, building support for systems change especially when increasing equity is an intentional goal, is tough. Most Americans (even those who work within these systems) often do not understand how those systems them were designed in the first place nor what redesigning would entail. Most of us are nervous about change generally (the fear of change is a notoriously tough challenge for changemakers to navigate) but it is especially challenging when people are genuinely unclear about how changing those systems would actually improve their lives. Essentially, when we say change, they hear, doom and gloom.

As a result, leaders seeking support for the kinds of systems changes that would produce more equitable outcomes, must work especially hard to make that case. One of the first challenges is to help make systems visible to people. Although people can clearly articulate the problems they see in their communities, they don't see the underlying systems. So, our first job is to make those systems visible – explaining what those systems do, why they are essential to everyday people's lives, and how they can be redesigned to function better for everybody.

The second challenge is that talking about "systems" without using all the jargon we've become accustomed to as leaders. We will need to master the ability to help people understand systems with as little jargon, technical language, or formal definition as possible. If our work is to make the case to technical audiences, they will already know something about the systems we are working to improve.

But because most of our casemaking will likely happen in front of people who lack that expertise and are unlikely to listen to long-winded explanations, we need the help of a heuristic device – something that helps break down information into smaller nuggets that our audiences can understand.

Specifically, this is a place where the use of an explanatory metaphor helps make a complicated system much easier to understand. Metaphors describing our systems can sound like this, *"our system functions like a vaccine, helping to protect families from negative outcomes"* or *"like smart cars helping our residents navigate the tough challenges they face in finding adequate health care or housing options"*. And, even the words "systems change" can function as its own kind of metaphor, especially when we use it to stand in for the world we want to shape. So, let's get busy wielding the powerful sword of metaphor!

Reflection Questions

- Am I making the systems that I want to change, visible and understandable in my conversations with stakeholders?
- Did I talk about what those systems do, how they function (and how they are malfunctioning or are challenged) by using an explanatory metaphor?
- Have I used the metaphors to help me explain why those systems are inequitable and consistently produce inequitable outcomes?
- Did I give specific examples of how changes in those systems will have practical benefits for people and will produce more equitable outcomes?

Your Ticket to Implementing This Principle

Two recommendations are key here: (1) use a metaphor to talk about the complex, overlapping systems that structure the outcomes we see in our communities and (2) use the opportunity of the systems metaphor to address the inequalities that our systems have created. By giving people a way to understand how systems produce equitable or inequitable outcomes, it helps them understand why our call-to-action is often about changing systems.

And, by giving people systemic context around the equity issues we raise, it helps them to locate the causes of inequality in systems (rather than the failings of the people we are trying to help). This is the perfect place in our casemaking to sharpen the lens on the inequalities caused by racism, sexism, ablism, individualism, homophobia and more.

Sample Success Measures

- [ ] **KPI:** We are consistently using a powerful metaphor that helps us explain why we need to redesign our systems of governance and how those systems produce racial, economic, and social inequity?
- [ ] **Outcome:** Our stakeholders are using our metaphor to describe the redesign our systems need and to describe the equitable outcomes we seek as a result?
- [ ] **Impact:** Our stakeholders are systems and equity focused; they understand that the "action" is in systems change and they are committed to solving the issues we face as systems issues.

USING METAPHORICAL THINKING TO MAKE SYSTEMS VISIBLE AND EMBED AN EQUITY LENS CONSTRUCTIVELY

Metaphors can be a powerful and important part of your casemaking. Generally, metaphors are powerful shortcuts that help people to understand complex structures like our health care system or our workforce development system, without the long-winded explanation experts usually offer. Because of this, metaphors can do the heavy lifting as you engage people about the systems change you hope to inspire, as well as help you build support for equity as part of your systems change work.

So, what's a metaphor and how do we use one in our work? Ever heard someone say, *"Time is money."* That's a metaphor. How often have you heard that statement? Probably many times and in various contexts. By thinking about time as money, you can create a powerful mental image that helps you (or others) reprioritize time. For many of us, we'd like to help people "reprioritize" how they view our work to reform the systems around us — especially those systems that are woefully out-of-date, reflect racist or sexist attitudes, and those that exacerbate problems or reinforce existing inequities.

What about these related metaphors? Ever heard these?

- **Time wasted is money down the drain.** (*emphasizes efficiency and the need to avoid waste*)
- **Time well spent is an investment.** (*emphasizes seeing time as a value, wanting to maximize that value, and the desire to see dividends or benefits from it*)
- **The seconds are ticking away.** (*emphasizes the urgency of the moment and how we measure that urgency – literally in increments of seconds*)

Each of these metaphors is working toward helping people reprioritize their time but each grabs a slightly different metaphor that reinforces a different aspect of time. This is important because the metaphor that you choose to use in your work should help you to convey the kind of systems change work that you are trying to do.

At their core, metaphors are really just fancy ways of comparing two unrelated or indirectly linked things. The visual mental picture that we get when a metaphor is used helps us boil down concepts to their most basic elements and engage in rapid sensemaking. The metaphors we use in casemaking work, by associating an unfamiliar idea with one that is commonplace, allows us to spark better understanding of complex ideas without the jargon we'd normally use.

Here are a few ways that metaphors can be helpful in your systems change work and some general metaphor examples to spark your creativity in making your case. Also, because we know that equity issues are best expressed as part of the systems metaphors, we offer some examples here on that as well.

Use a Metaphor to Break People Out of Their Fast Brains and Get Them into the <u>Slow Brain</u>! Often it is helpful to relate two things that seemingly have nothing to do with each other to break people out of their old ways of thinking about an issue. By breaking the rules of logic in this way, metaphors can open the creative, deliberative side of the brain – the part that is stimulated by images, ideas, brainstorming and new concepts. In this way, metaphorical thinking can help you "slow brain" the conversation and help people connect to their brainstorming and problem-solving power. To use another common metaphor, I'd say that metaphors help us *"think outside the box"*.

If you are using the metaphor to open up people's creative energy for thinking through solutions, don't get too hung up on how well the metaphor maps back. Metaphors that map too well can stifle the creativity you are trying to generate! The whole idea is to generate ideas, solutions, and reflections that you may not have otherwise thought of, so just let the ideas flow without too much scrutiny if your goal is ideation.

I use this technique in community meetings when I want stakeholders to think bigger about the possibilities for investment and development of their communities or neighborhoods. A good set of metaphors is a great way to focus your stakeholders on understanding exactly the kind of systems change we're after.

I will often offer up a bunch of metaphors on a white board and start by asking people to pick out the ones that most closely describe how their neighborhood or community operates today and then, ask them to pick a second one that best describes how _they'd like_ it to operate. Then, I ask them to try to see if they can come up with their own metaphors to describe their neighborhood and when they do, we start to try those metaphors on together.

Here are some examples:

Our community operates like a:
- a garden where it nurtures the people who live and work here

- a checkout line at the grocery store that moves very slowly, where we have plenty of time to talk to one another, but very little actual community-building gets done

- a factory where everybody has a job to do but they focus solely on that job and don't really see the whole community or have a holistic view of it

- an expensive jewelry store where the shopkeepers follow you around, and you do not feel welcome or like you ever really belong here

- a playground, where people are free to explore new things, connect constructively with neighbors and share community resources

Use a Metaphor to Explain Complex Systems, How They Work When They Function Well and How They Fail When We Are Not Vigilant About Updating or Repairing Them. Start here by using the metaphor to describe what the system is intended to do and then talk about why it has failed to live into that intention.

Here's an example: Most communities have the huge task of trying to align various parts of their education system with labor force opportunities. It is a daunting task to say the least. The best science about how to align well says that our systems need to be student-centered and coordinated across functions.

But our approach to education is often siloed in ways that make it more challenging for young people to have their needs holistically met. But what if our education system functioned more like a waterfall, moving students from one level to the next in a sequential way and linking each level directly to the next.

This kind of waterfall model would allow us to create an education-to-workforce development system that gave us the ability to better coordinate support to students at each level, measure their success, and focus on student-centered outcomes that are meaningful to both employers and educators at each level.

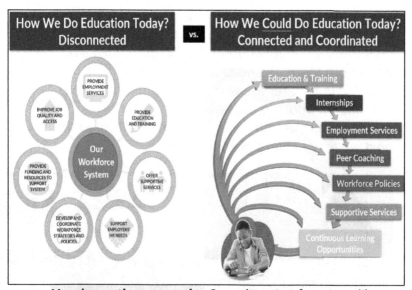

Here's another example: *Our education functions like a conveyor belt. It is supposed to move our students from elementary school through high school and then into careers. When it works well, the conveyor belt pushes people along at appropriate intervals as they achieve higher levels of proficiency. About 10 years ago, it started to sputter, graduating so few students from one grade level to the next, that it negatively affected our entire community.*

Few students were getting what they needed to move along, and they did not have the wherewithal to adjust. So today, our conveyor belt has come to a full stop, especially for the children who most need formal resources to achieve. Few students graduate and those that do, find themselves so unprepared for the available jobs that they quickly give up.

We need to rethink how our educational system prepares our children for success and make changes that adapt schools for the outcomes we need from them. We need a new conveyor belt – one that is built for the world we live in today. One that has the tools to prepare our children for success and that moves them from one level to the next, as they achieve proficiency.

Use a Metaphor When You Want to Identify Workable Solutions to System Problems. The solution ideas you have generated for the metaphorical problem can help your stakeholders find a workable solution to the real problem. By first talking about how systems are currently designed and secondarily how they are ill-designed to address the issues facing our communities today (in some way), we provide them with a mental framework to work from. Then we can ask about the kinds of solutions that might solve the metaphorical problem and ask, how might that apply to our real-world problem?

Here's an example: In the previous example about schools, we might ask them to talk about what a conveyor belt does and how it operates? What gives that mechanism power and what happens when it breaks down? How does it get fixed, who maintains it and how do we know when we need to replace it? Once they've answered those questions, then we ask them to apply what they know about conveyor belts to the real-world problem of graduation rates.

Here's another example: Racial segregation is a de facto rule in most communities across our nation. So much of how we invest in communities is still shaped by old, outdated bigoted practices that the time has come to rethink community investment. A well-functioning community investment system would not produce this much segregation, instead it would operate like a well-functioning regional transit system.

> *Transit systems provide open and shared access to the major roadways, central arteries and pathways across the region in a way that is more efficient than other more individualized modes of transportation. They connect people to local modes of transit and*

also to broader national modes of transportation (like Amtrak stations or airports). A well-functioning community investment system would offer the same kind of universal access, maximize efficiency, and connect communities to broader national investors or funding streams.

When a community investment system is working well, the system is visible to everyone (like transit maps); the system effectively fills gaps or mitigates those hard-to-reach places so that all communities have access to capital investments (like transit extenders or first/last mile options); and there are some players in the system who are "super-connectors" that ensure stability and efficiency (like transit stops that connect multiple transit lines together or weave together multiple modes of transport in multiple directions).

In the same way that most regions have come to understand the importance of creating an infrastructure to support transit, many are starting to understand the importance of organizing a well-functioning community investment system.

As our policymakers look to make high-return investments in our future, the work we do to build the infrastructure in our community investment system is critical.

We simply cannot adapt to the promising future in front of us if we continue to drag old issues like racial segregation with us. We need an infrastructure that allows us to adapt and move forward in an inclusive and equitable way.

We need an infrastructure that opens up new access to capital to invest in all communities across our region. That's how we change the imbalance of resources across communities, that's how we begin to address racial segregation, and that's how we ensure the pathway to opportunity.
Join us as we build the cross-sector, cross-community partnerships to build the community investment infrastructure in our region.

Metaphors are Also Helpful When You Want to Talk about Disparities Across Groups, Equity or Fairness but You Do Not Want to Reinforce Negative Stereotypes or to Engage in "Othering". When we lift up disparities across groups – like racial disparities in health outcomes or homeownership rates for example - if we are not careful to talk about those disparities in the context of the systems that created those disparities, we risk people making default assumptions about the groups we want to help. We risk provoking those dominant narratives about "individual responsibility" or the narrative of "racial difference", in a conversation where we want systems change to be centered.

No one doubts the incredible power of everyday people to overcome amazing and fantastic odds but no group of people should ever have to demonstrate odds-defying resilience to survive. We need systems to work better. So, when we use a systems metaphor and then talk about who has access to those systems, we spark a more constructive conversation. Let a strong metaphor help you do this heavy lifting.

Here's an example: Our housing system has evolved over time through a century of incremental changes. Some of these arose from policy decisions, others from the evolution of custom and practice. Evolutionary change can work well. But sometimes we see such profound changes to our environment that we need a deeper and more thought-out response in order to overcome a systemic problem. This is one of those times.

Our housing delivery system today operates like a five-gear manual transmission automobile. When the car works well, we have homes being built at all income levels (or at every gear): 1st gear serves people with very little income (often folks who are susceptible to homelessness); 2nd gear serves low-to moderate-income rental markets: 3rd gear serves high-end rental markets and 1st time homebuyers; 4th gear serves high-end real estate markets; and 5th gear serves commercial real estate needs.

Today however, our housing delivery system is not functioning well. In most regions of the country, our car is stuck in 3rd and 4th gears – producing very little housing beyond these two groups. A car operating in only two gears is not only incredibly inefficient (allowing safe travel on only a few roads) but is quite dangerous to everyone – the driver, the passengers, the pedestrians and the other cars on the road.

That's what has happened to housing in our country. Any mechanic would pull this car off the road for fear that it would endanger the wellbeing of many people. We need our policymakers to do the same. Pull this car (or our housing system) off the road for repair.

We need a housing system that doesn't put us all in jeopardy but rather, one that helps us all get stably housed. We need decisive action to redesign the housing delivery system so that it functions efficiently, works better for everyone, and produces diverse housing options for people at all income levels. Anything less puts us all in danger.

We need all five gears fully functional and operating. Because the first two gears are where the highest needs are, the initial work to improve the housing delivery system should start there – creating housing opportunities for people with very little income (but who still deserve a decent place to live) and those who are low-to-moderate-income renters.

These groups struggle the most to find affordable places to live because our housing system caters to those in higher income brackets. Historically, we have not served these two groups well – racial and income discrimination, redlining, restrictive covenants, and other system barriers have made it more difficult for the gears to work effectively, able to meet the growing housing needs of our residents.

Thus, we need to redefine success so that we understand that our system is operating effectively when people in first and second gears have as much access to housing, as people in any other group (or gear). In other words, only a housing system that ensures access to people in the lower end of the income spectrum can claim to be working optimally.

This is urgent and important work. Help us as we rethink how we provide housing resources across the country, as we modify policies, increase investment, and focus immediate housing assistance on the millions of families not being well-served today.

Take the time to read through the detailed plan on our website, offer your support for this work, and help us intentionally plan for a housing system that gets our car "in gear", operating at peak performance for everybody.

Use Your System Metaphors to Convey the Need to Grow, Scale or Better Deliver Solutions that Are Working. Metaphors are great mechanisms for helping to convey how and why your solution works best as well as for communicating the need to grow the reach and scale of that solution. So, if the case that you are making is about the need to elevate a solution or to advance the need to invest in and scale something that is already working, a metaphor might help you do that.

Here's an example: *Women are critical to the advancement of all communities, but women's contributions are especially important in nations that experience high levels of poverty. In the 1920s, the Ghanaian scholar James Emman Aggrey said, "If you educate a man you simply* educate an individual, but if you educate a woman, you educate a whole nation."

A World Bank study found that every year of secondary school education is correlated with an 18 percent increase in a girl's future earning power. And research shows that educating girls has a multiplier effect. Better-educated women tend to be healthier, participate more in the formal labor market, earn more, give birth to fewer children, marry at a later age, and provide better health care and education to their children.

Investing in women is like **a ripple effect** – it not only helps the woman involved but it also prospers the entire community.

INVEST IN GIRLS AND WOMEN:
THE RIPPLE EFFECT

IMPROVE HEALTH

Women who use maternal health services are more likely to use other reproductive health services, and to seek health care for their children.

BENEFIT FAMILIES

Girls and women spend 90% of their earned income on their families, while men spend only 30–40%.

GIRLS & WOMEN ARE AT THE HEART OF DEVELOPMENT

When 10% more girls go to school, a country's GDP increases by an average of 3%.

STRENGTHEN ECONOMIES

INCREASE PRODUCTIVITY

Eliminating barriers to employment for girls and women could raise labor productivity by 25% in some countries.

{ INVESTING IN GIRLS AND WOMEN WILL... }

Growing evidence shows that corporations led by women are more focused on sustainability.

CREATE SUSTAINABLE NATIONS

REDUCE HUNGER

Closing the gender gap in agriculture could lift 100–150 million people out of hunger.

WOMEN DELIVER

WHO WINS? EVERYBODY.

Use Your System Metaphors to Help People Understand the Value of Your Organization, Coalition, Agency or Group to Leading the System Change Effort. As part of your work to underscore how systems function (and malfunction), how they can be improved and the work to redesigned them, take the time to share how your team fits into the work. We talk more explicitly about sharing your value proposition in Principle #9 later in this book but you can get started by positioning your team as part of the system metaphor that you create.

Here's an example: *Our coalition operates like a flywheel (or simply a wheel built on an axis that stores energy that can be redistributed). Flywheels preserve momentum so well that the energy*  *stakeholders add to spin it faster in one part of the system, adds more to the capacity of the whole system. We are working to ensure that the energy we spend gathering and feeding insights from our community health practitioners back into the system, helps us to target and resolve the biggest points of friction across our health system. Together we are the flywheel that ensures better service delivery in our system and improved health outcomes for everybody.*

Rules of Thumb for Crafting and Using Metaphors

There is no "right metaphor" – the ideas can be as unrelated as you like. But there are some general tips for making sure that your use of metaphor works well in the case that you are making.

1. **Make sure your metaphors are understandable and instantly ring true with your audience.** If people cannot understand the relationship between the two things you are relating, it won't help you very much. So, calibrate the metaphor to the group to which you are making your case.

2. **Be clear about what it is about the system that you want to change and use the metaphor to describe that.** Are you working to change its delivery or financing model? Are you working to address racism or other inequities caused by how the system operates today? Perhaps you are working to better connect community residents or industry consumers to the solutions? Perhaps you are working to operationalize equity by embedding a racial equity lens or health impact lens or another kind of lens, into the decision-making process?

Whatever the goal of your system change effort, the metaphor you choose should help you highlight that kind of change. Once you are clear about what about the system you are trying to change (i.e., where change is needed to improve and grow more equitable outcomes), then you can work on metaphors that help you to say that simply.

3. **Think of other instances in life where that same characteristic, idea, emotion, state, etc. applies.**

   - You may be trying to get your stakeholders to understand that you are accelerating the pace of innovation (*maybe a race car or rocket ship metaphor*)

   - You may be helping to connect those stakeholders to valuable resources (*maybe wiring, telephone or Wi-Fi are metaphors that help you*)
   - Perhaps, you are describing the kind of collaborative spirit you are working to develop with your strategic partners (*sports team, orchestra or other team building metaphors*).

Whatever it is, identify the kind of change that you are working toward and choose metaphors that tell that story.

4. **There may be many metaphors for the situation you are describing – test a couple of related metaphors out to see how well they relate to your audience.** Once you've done some creative work to think about what system change you are trying to create, test a couple metaphors to ensure they work well with the people you are talking to. Informally, you can test them with your stakeholders to gauge their reactions directly or you can hire formal researchers to test a series of related metaphors to see which work best for the groups you are trying to engage.

The Smart Car of Community Development

Over the last 20 years, community developers have worked hard to advance more equitable development and healthy communities. Yet without stronger investment in our infrastructure (our ability to meet the changing environment around us), our power to impact the lives of those who need us most, is limited.

As we watch economic inequality rise, climate disasters happen repeatedly, housing affordability moves out of reach of average Americans, the stakes are higher, and the journey to opportunity, is made more challenging. When these emergent challenges are coupled with the long-standing structural and institutional barriers that have curtailed opportunity, especially within communities of color, we are made even more aware of just how critical our work is to invest in our communities.

Shouldering the historic legacies of racism and bigotry that have stripped households and communities of wealth does not have to continue to be the path of our nation. This is unjust and our investment in burrowing a different pathway should be one of our nation's highest priorities.

The good news is that we have more knowledge, information, and opportunities to help. That's why our work to provide our version of **the smart car** for a field that is still driving ineffective back-office functions, needs stronger support. Our service specifically addresses some of the toughest challenges we face as a nation by strengthening the capacity of community developers and bringing new resources to communities that have historically faced disinvestment.

Like a smart car, we work to advance the navigation systems of our field. We provide strategic guidance that helps seasoned community leaders do what they do best (drive programs and services to assist residents) but with the benefit of assistance in key areas like human resources, accounting, and other back-office functions. As independent non-profits, each member remains in the driver's seat setting its own destination; we assist with navigation providing high-level program expertise and leadership.

Under the hood, our back-end administrative services ensure that its members see the road ahead clearly, remain focused on what's ahead in their lanes, and can travel as efficiently as possible. When our drivers (partner CDCs) have the freedom to focus on their mission, strategies, and impact, their journey is easier, and their work is more impactful.

Navigating Our Way to Better Community Outcomes:
Helping Community Development Corporations to Drive Better Outcomes

Level 0
CDCs are struggling with back-office functions with limited support.

Level 1
CDCs have support for basic administrative functions.

Level 2
CDCs have support for basic administrative functions, human resources & grants management.

Level 3
CDCs have support for basic administrative functions, human resources, grants management, & program evaluation.

Level 3
CDCs have support for basic administrative functions, human resources, grants management, program evaluation, & overall portfolio management.

Without Support

More Impact With Critical Supports

# Principle #7: Tell the Story of Us

Stories are so powerful. Research shows that in storytelling mode, we sit, listen, and think differently. Stories make information easier to understand and to digest. Studies have also shown that people recall information more easily when it is shared via stories than when people are given facts alone. Stories are also better at holding people's attention (because a good story gets people interested in how it unfolds).

Yet many of the stories that we are sharing to try to generate support for our work, leave out: (1) the stakeholders whose support we need, (2) those with lived experience of the issues we are trying to tackle, and (3) the systems that we are trying to change. As a result, we unwittingly leave people to their best guess when they try to fit themselves into the story we are asking them to participate in. Without some direction, they have to ascertain what THEIR responsibility is in solving the adaptive challenge we've outlined. Then, we leave them to guess again about whether our call-to-action has anything at all to do with their lives or our ability to solve this issue.

So, our task is to harness the power of storytelling by including our stakeholders, our systems and those with lived experience in our stories.

We can tell all kinds of interesting, vivid, asset-based stories as long as they are strategic – serving the goal to build broader public will around the case that we are making, by limiting the social distance around the issue.

Rethinking Our Stories
In the social justice space, we often tell stories about the individuals who need help, to draw people into a bigger conversation about the systemic change we are trying to make. Or we invite people to tell their own stories to help them feel the power in their voice and build a bigger movement.

Here's the problem: Research shows that stories that focus on people's individual circumstances tend to move us in the direction of trying to "fix" those individual circumstances. We might ask, *"Can I give a small donation to that family? Can I pray with the family or for the children? Can I bring canned goods or run a toy drive for the children?"*

While there's nothing wrong with those offerings, they won't transform the world we live in over the long term. If we're really after justice, even well-intended charity won't cut it. We need our systems to deliver for us, and our stories should reflect that.

Here are a couple ground rules to help you do that!

Center the experiences of people who are directly impacted in your communities. Make space for people to narrate their own stories and encourage them to do so authentically, speaking truth to power. Encourage them to include the ways in which the systems around them supported or undermined their ability to thrive. The latter are the places where we are likely to have the most impactful casemaking, if we get the story right!

Make people AND systems the main characters in your stories. Tell fascinating stories about the ways our education, health care, housing, and workforce systems make a difference in people's lives and the ways that we need those systems to be reimagined to deliver a better tomorrow for all of us.

Direct attention to the dignity, strength, and resilience of the people in your stories, and remind us of how we ALL benefit when everybody in our communities has what they need to thrive. Don't describe what's wrong with people and where they live — that only invites othering and exclusion. Lead with language that invites people to a conversation about our strengths and tell stories about how our systems could make us even stronger.

Tell visionary, future-oriented stories about the way our systems could be operating to help us meet the future. We all know that most of the systems that are meant to keep us strong in our communities are in deep crisis. It doesn't help to keep reminding people of that. Help people see that there are already real-world solutions and all we need to do is mobilize our communities to lift them up.

Finally, a good story is one that excites, surprises, helps us lean in to see what happens, and leaves us wanting more. That means using all the means of telling a compelling and engaging story. Sometimes this means using different modalities to tell the story (video, metaverse, interpretative dance, spoken word, and more) as well as good techniques of surprise, wonder and amazement. That's a tall order but essential if you want to get (and keep) people's attention.

Remember, you're competing with Netflix, YouTube, Tik Tok and all the rest – for people's precious few minutes of down time. So, let's engage people constructively!

Reflection Questions

- Am I giving space so that people who are most affected by the solutions I'm advocating for, get to tell their story?
- When I share stories about the solution, am I centering those with lived experience? Am I sharing their stories in ways that start with their humanity, dignity, resilience, and the systems that should be helping them to maintain those traits?
- Am I widening the circle of people who see themselves as part of the problem and solution (some of whom may not have thought about how much they are affected by or implicated in this problem or its solution)?
- Am I using different modalities to tell stories about the solutions (video, social media, poems, music, art, etc.)?
- Am I telling stories that are compelling and put people in our collective future?
- Am I using storytelling to get people to wonder, question, dream, and feel inspired about what we can achieve together?

Your Ticket to Implementing This Principle

Storytelling allows us to engage and reach people differently. Stories give us the opportunity to be creative, to use humor, wit, vivid images, metaphors and to tap into people's empathy and emotion.

So, take advantage of that opportunity. Tell the story of your work and who it benefits in entirely different ways; with faces and places that people would never have associated with your issue. Most of all, get creative! A good story uses all of our creative juices to get people engaged.

Sample Success Measures

☐ **KPI:** We are consistently telling stories that grab people differently, centering lived experience, systems, and new stakeholders. We are telling stories about people's dignity, strengths, and resilience – and how our systems should be protecting those traits. We are telling stories that allow more people to see themselves as part of the solution.

☐ **Outcome:** Our stakeholders have more empathy for people with lived experience; they see themselves and systems as part of the story; they start to share their own stories about how they too are affected by the problems and solutions we have lifted up.

☐ **Impact:** New stakeholders are supporting our work; they have a stronger commitment and understanding of the work that we are doing; and they value people who have lived experience as integral parts of the conversation and solutions. People feel more stake in the solutions and retell the story with themselves in it.

WAKE UP PEOPLE!
Getting to the Slow Brain

Over the last 20 years, more people have become interested in psychologists' exploration of the two modes of thinking people use to process information. We might call them the fast and the slow brain (in deference to the acclaimed psychologist and Nobel prize winner Daniel Kahneman and his book, *Thinking Fast and Slow*).

The fast brain operates automatically and quickly, with little or no effort and no sense of voluntary control. This is the part of the brain that people use to respond to us when we approach them about supporting our work. This fast brain doesn't take us very seriously – it quickly dispatches with us, doesn't use much mental processing power to evaluate our claims, think through our solutions, nor think deeply about how to react to our call-to-action. Don't take it personal, it's just our brain's way of processing information super-fast.

The slow brain, on the other hand, is the one we want. The slow brain is the part of the brain that allocates attention, allows us to focus and perform more complex mental functions. This slow brain is the one that is more deliberative, and engages people's sense of agency, choice, and concentration. The slow brain allows people a chance to really think about what we're saying and to reconsider the old/bad information they might have stored in their thinking.

Having people stuck in fast brain mode is problematic for us. So, our challenge (and opportunity) is to literally kick people out of the fast brain and into the slow brain. There are many ways to do this, but the easiest way is often to grab their attention in a creative or unexpected way, literally forcing them to stop and reconsider what you've said or presented. Using humor or unusual methods of engaging people can force them to stop, for just a moment, to really process what you are trying to do and to have them engage differently.

For example, a few years ago, there was the ice-bucket challenge that brought awareness to an important medical condition (ALS) and raised more than $115 million from all over the world. It was one of the most successful fundraising efforts in the history of nonprofit fundraising and it was successful not just because it raised money but because it "slow brained" people. It engaged them differently, in a relatively meaningless but fun activity, that went viral. It gave the nonprofit just enough time and space to open people up differently than if they had a formal fundraising appeal.

Similarly, the Nature Rx campaign uses an eye-catching and unusual way to remind people that many of the psychological "disorders" we suffer from today could be solved by...nature! That is, so many of the things that are ailing us are really about not having enough time for self-care and could be solved relatively inexpensively by having people spend more time outdoors, in green settings, mostly getting away from work or stress producing activities, to really enjoy the outdoors. Their online ads imitate pharmaceutical commercials in a funny and sarcastic way that engages people differently – kicking people into the slow brain for just enough time to have them stop and consider the impact of nature on their mental and physical health.

Another example, the Broccoli versus Kale campaign (The Broccoli Makeover) sponsored by the New York Times used a fictitious rivalry between two vegetables to expand public consumption of Broccoli. The ad team assigned to the campaign decided to "pick a fight with Kale" (a much cooler vegetable) to get more attention to the consumption of vegetables.

They created a fictitious Broccoli Commission of America, whose slogans include: *"Broccoli: Now 43 Percent Less Pretentious Than Kale"* and *"What Came First, Kale or the Bandwagon?"* and *"Eat Fad Free: Broccoli v. Kale."* Picking on kale — rather than on, say, French fries — was especially brilliant because it mimicked the Great Soda War between Pepsi and Coca-Cola in the 1980s, an entirely bloodless battle that greatly enhanced the bottom lines of both companies.

Some of the local versions of the Broccoli campaign created t-shirts, hats, buttons, other paraphernalia, and sister ads to support the campaign. Most important, the ad campaign is said to have grown public consumption of broccoli by more than 102%. This wasn't just "creative marketing", it was about slow braining the content for consumers who were not likely to pay attention to a traditional conversation about the merits of broccoli or any other vegetable.

If you are working on an issue that needs more attention, master the fine art of getting people to the slow brain – the place where they have to (and maybe they even WANT to) stop and figure out what you're talking about!

Samples of "slow brain" campaign of the Broccoli Makeover

<u>Some context about this example first:</u> To bring public attention to the need to invest in beach restoration across the state, we worked with a statewide coalition to send postcards to legislators from the beach reminding them of how much our beaches are not only our playgrounds but bring in significant revenue for the state. Without attention to beach erosion, those things are in jeopardy. The post cards were one part of our campaign. We then had our advocates across the state put pictures on their social media pages from their vacations at various beaches across the state and tag legislators. The response was swift – we got legislators to pay attention and prioritize funds for beach restoration projects across the state. Here's a snapshot at what we sent and said.

 ### Twenty Years Ago, We Were All Swimming at Our Beaches. Now We're Swimming Upstream to Save Them.

Ten years ago, would have been a great time for a few strong, decisive steps to improve the quality, condition, and care of our beaches. Ten years ago, the first state-wide beach erosion report was released, and scientists warned that without significant intervention to care for the natural environment of our beaches, that we could literally lose them.

Ten years ago, none of this seemed as serious as it does today.
The world around us has changed quickly in the years since the first erosion report was
released. The pollutants, the over-fishing and farming upstream, increased tourism and global warming, have all contributed to the need to adapt our response to caring for our beaches.

Without strong, decisive, coordinated action across the state, the condition of our beaches will continue to erode, worsening the experience for our tourists, dragging down our quality of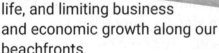
life, and limiting business and economic growth along our beachfronts.

But here's the good news. If the amount of time we spend on our beaches is any indication of how much we love our outdoors, our environment and our beaches, then our work to gather support to invest in them should be easy. With science on our side, unprecedented momentum from our state legislators and beach front coalitions actively engaging people across our state, we are now ready to take coordinated, decisive action.

Ten years ago, we were not ready but today offers us another, better pathway. 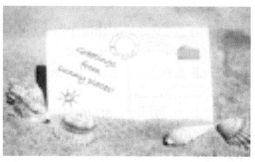 Today, we act with strong, shared purpose on an issue that affects us all.

The investment that we need to make in our environment is made from a recognition of our shared history, our strength, our adaptive leaders, and our desire to responsibly grow our state's economy.

The statewide initiative leading the charge on this issue was created to map the path to that better future, where we all continue to have access to the beautiful beaches we love, as well as to the restaurants and hotels that support tourism.

We'll do our work in this initiative by engaging voices throughout the state, and sharing expertise from all over, in this effort. We will put each unique beach community's preservation priorities front and center, while learning from the best of what other communities across the state are doing already. And we'll use that input to guide and measure our progress along the way.

It won't be easy. We're a state of complexity and contrasts: downtowns and suburbs and rural areas; tourists, transplants, and multi-generational families; businesses, academia, government, nonprofits, and faith communities; many cultural backgrounds, many languages, many types of different homes and circumstances, with different needs and uses for our beaches.

Yet, no matter who we are or where we live in our state, we all enjoy and depend on our beaches in some way. Now, our beaches need something from all of us in return. We need everybody and all these voices engaged and pulling together – and dissenting sometimes too – to transform our shared future. We know what the consequences are of doing nothing, and it's not what we want for our environment or our beaches.

THE story OF us

We need your postcards of love from our beaches, your stories, numbers, data, policies, dollars, expertise, capacity, organizations, and government agencies, of course. But most of all?

We need YOU. This is your home. The beaches are yours.

Welcome to the team. Get involved!

Principle #8: Foster Collective Ownership

In the work that I do with my team, we often conduct community voice sessions to hear first-hand how people understand the social challenges in front of us. We're listening for a variety of things in those conversations – one of the most important of which are the personal narratives that people use to justify why they are not more active on social justice issues. That is, we listen carefully to how people move from being passionately opinionated about how the world should work, to explaining why they put no effort into making sure that our world lives into their vision. In essence, we listen to people explain their journey into bystander status in their own lives.

Have you ever stopped to wonder why people in our country have such strong, passionate opinions about the challenges happening in our world today but aren't at all involved in making things better?

Part of the issue is **learned helplessness**. While I hate the term "learned helplessness", what it describes is an important impediment to action that has implications for how we mobilize bystanders into action.

Learned helplessness is simply the phenomenon that as we are continually exposed to situations where we either have no decision-making power (or perceive that we have no power), we stop trying to exert control over those situations. If we don't believe that our actions will change things, why try? Essentially, we become resigned to the idea that we'd better just get used to the status quo and do what we can to survive in it, rather than change it.

So, for example, if we start to see more people experiencing homelessness in our community and we don't perceive that we have any power to solve that problem, we rail against the problem but don't put much energy into a solution.

And perhaps most important, to justify our decision to remain bystanders, we take up a narrative that helps us explain why we aren't doing more than put a few dollars into the tin cup of the people we meet on the street. In my work across the country, the most common narrative I hear to justify bystander status is the *"have and have nots"* narrative – where people explain that they are part of the "have nots" class in our nation and so any of their efforts to change the circumstances around them will be met with counter force by people who have much more power and influence. Why try to fight those who have so much more power?

With that narrative in place, most people don't try for something better, and we don't contribute our time and talent to organizations trying to change the status quo. Rather, we resort back to one of two bookend narratives – either **bad government** or **personal responsibility**. Neither of which moves us forward. Because of how common and calcified these narratives are, it warrants an extended conversation about these two companion narratives.

In the public discourse of most social problems in our nation today, we are bookended by two competing and equally undermining dominant narratives. On the first of the two bookends is the narrative that **government is responsible for solving all social problems** and at the same time, **government is too corrupt and inefficient to solve those problems**.

At the other bookend is the second narrative - **individual or personal responsibility.** That narrative can sound a bit like this - *"those people need to take personal responsibility for what's happening to them, it's not my problem"* or *"it's not my responsibility to take care of somebody else's kids, take care of your own"*.

There are other harmful dominant narratives in our culture that hold us back from seizing our collective strength, but these two tend to be the most common and damaging. They harm our ability to mobilize people who feel empowered enough to decide what their communities could and should look like or how they want their own communities to feel.

In particular, the "bad government" narrative allows us to displace responsibility on an entity that cannot possibly solve these issues in isolation. In that respect, the bad government narrative is a self-fulfilling prophecy. Government cannot solve what is ailing our nation – not in isolation or consensus from a wide range of community actors. So, in essence, we give the problems we face to government to solve (something we see as outside of ourselves) and then complain that government can't solve the problems that we've just assigned to it. Insanity? Absolutely!

The narratives about individual or personal responsibility are equally unhelpful. While it is true that we need to hold people accountable for their choices, too often their choices are limited by larger systemic issues that offer them few choices to begin with. Blaming people for the circumstances in which they find themselves may be akin to blaming people for the failures of our systems.

Not only is that unproductive and unfair but it can demoralize the very people who are closest to the problems we seek to solve and those we most need to engage in social action.

Because the systems around us shape so many of the outcomes we see playing out in communities, we have to be able to toggle between holding our government accountable and holding ourselves accountable. Yet in a culture that valorizes the extremes at both narrative bookends, it has been difficult to hold this tension in hand. But that is exactly the task. In our casemaking, we have to hold ourselves accountable for making the decision to own the problems we face and their solutions.

Let me say this even more directly, we will only solve the challenges in front of us by getting the everyday heroes in our community (and by heroes, I mean everyone in our community) to take ownership of what we do together. That means using our casemaking to shift people out of bystander status by getting around learned helplessness. It also means navigating around the dominant narratives that are impediments to mobilizing people to action. We are the ones we've been waiting for and we have to own the decision-making to do so.

Our casemaking has to change the energy – we have to mobilize people who have already decided that it's not in their interests to fight for change. We have to help them connect to their power to change the world because we actually do have the authority and power (as owners of the problem and its solutions) to decide what actions we will take together. How we show up in this moment, in every moment, is actually what matters.

Mobilizing people in the service of collective action means that we have to shift power. The power is no longer in the hands of government, or corporations, or even our individual selves. The real power is in our collective decisions to work together to solve what is ours to do. The first step on that journey is to help people find and connect to the power in their own voices. So let's talk about how we do that!

Talking People Back into Their Power

To change the systems that urgently need our support, we'll need to get people in their communities — community residents, people in community organizations, government, and industry — to see their agency. That is, we need to talk them back into the power they have given up and navigate around the dominant narratives about government and individual responsibility.

Here's how we can begin to address the learned helplessness that people feel and turn our bystanders into active stakeholders.

Help people remember a time when everyday people won. On the news and social media and in popular culture, we're bombarded with stories that remind us of how bad things are. We are told constantly about injustices, crises, tragedies and predatory institutions that feel too big for us to fight and win. It's no wonder people don't immediately respond to our calls to action. We must remind people of the times when ordinary people joined with others in their communities and, despite incredible odds, did something extraordinary: solved a problem, built a school, forced city council to do something different, got a corporate leader to provide community benefits or share in profits. Those things are happening constantly, but they seldom make the nightly news. That's why we have to tell THOSE stories!

Position everyday people as decision-makers. For a variety of reasons, most of us have come to think only government and corporate leaders have the decision-making power on the issues that matter most. So, we must help ordinary people connect to their power as decision-makers. That may mean different things in different contexts, but the objective is to put power in the hands of everyday people who have the expertise, motivation, integrity and skills to follow through on issues that are meaningful to the community. Say, *"The landscape of our community is being decided today. The decisions we make today will determine our future. Our future needs us today!"*

Then, make sure people understand how they can participate in those decisions.

'We are the ones we've been waiting for.' This statement sounds like a cliché, but it's true, and it spurs people to action. Remind people that there is no knight in shining armor who is coming to save us. The only "saving" that will happen is through people working to advance a better future for themselves and their communities. Say, *"There is no one coming to save us but us. We are the ones we've been waiting for."*

It also helps when people remember that they are not alone on the journey. Talk about the many people, groups, local businesses, organizations and institutions that are doing their part to contribute to the solution. Then help people figure out what their unique contribution will be and see why their contribution is so critical to the whole.

Reflection Questions

- Did I make it clear that this is an issue that is OUR responsibility to solve and that we own the solutions?
- Did I make it clear that we must decide our collective future together and that government is only one of many actors that we need to direct?

- Did I talk people into their power by reminding them of past examples where they worked with others in their communities to solve big things?
- Did I position my audience as heroes in a story of many heroes in my community?
- Did I make it clear that by using concrete examples that we all benefit from solving this issue as a community concern?

Your Ticket to Implementing This Principle

When you want to motivate people who are now bystanders, take the time to ask them to remember when ordinary people achieved extraordinary things in their community. Get a running tally of examples that are commonly known and understood in your community. Then, before you get to any call-to-action, make it a point to reference the things on that list with as many details and appreciative inquiry as you can.

Ask questions like, "do you all remember when we charged the hill, got that done, challenged what wasn't working for us in this community"? Ask people to recall how it worked before in those circumstances and then ask them to put the same energy into the issue that you are trying to mobilize them around. It will make all the difference in the response that you get!

Sample Success Measures

- ☐ **KPI:** We are consistently reinforcing that we own the solutions to this problem, government's role is minimized, and we are talking people back into their power using the techniques outlined here.

- ☐ **Outcome:** Our stakeholders are describing this issue as OUR responsibility to solve and about the benefits WE reap from solving it.

- ☐ **Impact:** Our stakeholders see the resolution of this issue as inextricably connected to their own social and economic wellbeing.

DEALING WITH THE DOMINANT NARRATIVES ABOUT GOVERNMENT: CROWDING OUT THE NEGATIVE TALK

Let's tackle the challenge that stumps even the best and well-resourced efforts to advance systems change in the United States today – the role of government! This issue is as old as they come – our country was founded by people challenging the role for government, so it stands to reason that even today, if you are going to activate people to change the world around them, you have to position the role of government very carefully and effectively. What is the best role for government? How big or small should government be and what are the consequences of changing government's role in ensuring a standard of living for all Americans?

Over the last 30 years, in particular, our notion of "government" has taken a beating in the public imagination. From former President Reagan's harmful and consistent definition of government as "the problem itself", to his skillful wielding of the "welfare queen" caricature, he sewed a negative public assessment of government into the very fabric of our public discourse. Reagan's painting of government programs as wasteful and spending on the "undeserving" was so successful that it continues to invade all public conversations about what government can and should be able to do.

But to be fair, it would be wrong to assume that it was only Reagan beating this drum - similar narratives exist on both the progressive left and conservative right that demonize our government for exacerbating a host of problems that continue to plague our nation. And, many of those assessments (like the role our government has played in creating racially segregated housing and neighborhoods) cannot be denied. They are true.

Luckily our task in our casemaking is not to resolve how people perceive government. You likely have enough already on your plate and do not need the additional lift of having to save how we see government. Yet, if we are to be effective in making a case for change, we will have to grapple with how to effectively position government in our narrative. So here's the deal.

Today, there is such an enormous amount of cynicism about solving the scale of the larger adaptive challenges we face (like poverty, affordable housing, health care, education, etc.) and people's support often gets hung up in their negative assessments of government. That is, people generally assign the bigger challenges to "government" to solve and when our government institutions cannot single-handedly solve these challenges, the failure reinforces the default perception that government is to blame and cannot be a constructive agent of change.

This is really a shame because while our government may in fact have its issues, we also have to acknowledge that we have not always given our governmental leaders the "best hand" (or the best tools and resources) for it alone to solve any of the adaptive challenges we face. That is, the solutions we need require the alignment of all sectors and a great number of institutional partners and stakeholders. Getting that level of cooperation and stakeholder alignment is tough. But more important, it literally means that not much is possible around issues of equity unless more of us are leaning forward.

The casemaking challenge for those of us working to solve truly adaptive problems, is that government is a necessary and important partner. Yet, for many Americans, "government as an agent of positive change", is a nonstarter.

This is important because so much of the public opposition we hear related to contemporary public policy proposals, fall short under the weight of this now fairly common belief that government is part of the problem and cannot be part of the solution.

This presumption means that our government (which most people see as outside of themselves), simply cannot be made to ever operate in the best interests of everyday citizens. The fact that our current political system feels like it is in full meltdown, with so much polarization and in-fighting, reinforces this all-too-common perception.

This creates a dangerous dynamic where we rail against government, become bystanders in our own lives, and then ask people to support our efforts to embrace government (through policymakers) to create better outcomes! Or alternatively, we do not ask much of our government or our leaders because we assume their incompetence and inability to solve problems, that are clearly too large for us working alone to shoulder.

Let's face it – most of us feel overwhelmed by all of the so-called crises that seem to be happening simultaneously around us and it's just easier to deposit all of that stuff at the feet of government leaders and then complain because they (alone) cannot fix it.

**To navigate around the "bad government"
narrative and activate bystanders to get involved,
we have to be strategic. Here's how.**

**We have to master the fine art of crowding out
"government" as the agent of change in our
stories.** We start by telling bigger "stories of us"
(that is, stories of shared responsibility, obligation
and sacrifice for the broader whole of our
communities). Telling stories of shared
responsibility, where we divide responsibility for
solving adaptive challenges across a wide array of
community leaders, organizations and institutions,
reinforces a bigger message about the value of
each. And, it has the added benefit of crowding
out government as the primary (or only) source of
change.

**Start the call-to-action by explicitly saying
something like this:** *The only way this issue will be
resolved is if you and I make it happen. There is no
calvary coming to save us. There is no one group or
organization, no agency or messiah coming with all
the reinforcements we need. There are no quick and
easy solutions. There is no government agency or
corporation with a silver bullet. This is hard work
and we will all need to roll up our sleeves to enable
the change we want to see.*

Then, call for the question by saying something like this: *Here's what the banks are doing to help ____. Here's what the hospitals are starting to do to help ____. Here's what the YMCA, Boys and Girls Clubs, Urban League, United Way and other community led organizations are doing to help____. Here's what our corporate partners are doing to help ____. Here's what I'm doing to help. The only question is what will you contribute to help?*

Then, reinforce the value of their unique contribution by saying something like this: *I'm glad you can help in this way. We literally would not be able to solve this without you. Are there others in your social network – your friends, family, co-workers, neighbors, kids teachers or coaches, that you could help us engage and get them involved? We need as much help and support as we can get?*

Then, bring government back in by saying something like this: *And, we will make progress so much faster if we ask additional corporate, governmental, nonprofit and community leaders to lean forward as well. We all have a unique role to play. We need corprate leaders to do even more by____, we need governmental leaders (at all levels) to do more by ____, we need nonprofits to do more by____, we need community leaders to do more by ____. Systems only change when we are all working together to make change happen and when we are united in our direction.*

Most people (although not all) will offer to contribute in some way, once they know that others in their same community have contributed something. What often stops people from leaning forward is when they feel like there isn't a real shared sacrifice.

So our task is to position shared sacrifice first (no matter how small those initial sacrifices of others may be) and then to ask for people's contribution as well. Once we've been able to get them out of bystander mode and mindset (because they can see the sacrifices others are already making), then together we can advocate for better governmental policies. The latter, of course, is the bigger ask.

The strategy here is to crowd out the negative talk about government that happens when the case that we are making allows people to displace the problems on government. Some of those problems may be exacerbated by government but they cannot and will not be solved WITHOUT government. **So, positioning government as merely one actor in a much larger set of actors is key, if our goal is to get people to take action, responsibility and agency for the adaptive challenges we face.**

This casemaking principle is likely to be one of the

toughest in practice because we have become so accustomed to villainizing government. Yet if you don't position these leaders as partners, not only do you ensure that you won't get their partnership but you won't be able to move broader public audiences to action. They'll stay stuck in villainizing others, which may be cathartic but doesn't help us move the needle on anything!

Also be clear, this strategy does not mean that you cannot have a healthy critique of government leaders. But it means that if your goal is to inspire people to "get off the fence and pitch in to help", a long, ongoing negative diatribe about government is unlikely to help. It will instead have the opposite effect. In an environment where people are so polarized and distrustful already, having you pile more critique on, only serves to undermine the eventual deals that you'll need to broker with those governmental leaders, if you are to be successful.

Instead, if you have a critique of government, state it clearly and unequivocally, then follow it up directly with a series of reasons why you believe this moment is a unique opportunity to partner more effectively than ever, with a whole range of leaders including governmental leaders, agencies and institutions.

This rule holds true as well with other types of leaders whose partnership is necessary for your work. If a strong critique is necessary, state it explicitly then, follow it directly with what gives you optimism that the partnership you need in those leaders can and will emerge. If you're not able to get there – to a place where you have a positive way to shape the partnership you'll need with those leaders you want to critique, it is unlikely that you will get other people (those bystanders) to lean forward to support your work. Think of it in this way – with all of the fighting and calamitous tension in the world today, who wants to be joined into a cat fight? They'd rather be heroes in a story about creating the communities they envision for themselves and their families.

Our City, Our Future: Together, We Will Decide Our Future

Over the last twenty years, we've made extraordinary progress in revitalizing neighborhoods across our city. And here's the thing: none of it was inevitable or could have happened without the extraordinary collaboration we have experienced. We have worked across sectors, creating stronger partnerships than ever before. We have needed every business, every resident, every nonprofit, every city agency and our national partners working with us, to do this well. It was the result of tough choices we made together, and the result of your hard work and resilience.

Now, the task to keep us moving forward is one that falls to all of us, as well. Sustaining and building on all we've achieved – from having mortgage lenders develop customized programs for families in targeted areas, to developers hiring more young people in the building trades as they create more affordable housing, to our corporate partners helping us to invest in shovel-ready projects, to our city agencies protecting our drinking water and storm-water management, to our nonprofits contributing new playgrounds for our kids – that's going to take all of us continuing to work together.

Because that's always been our story – the story of ordinary people, conscious employers, caring nonprofits, civic organizations and our city government coming together in the hard, slow, sometimes frustrating, but always vital work of self-governing.

Here's what we have learn for sure. Having dilapidated neighborhoods in a city as prosperous and innovative as we are, just doesn't make sense. We decided long ago that poverty and blight are too expensive for us. The loss of human potential, the hopelessness of those living in crime-ridden neighborhoods and the health consequences – all come at a price much too high for us to pay.

Why allow poverty and blight to be facts of life for so many in our city when we have the power to prevent and perhaps even, eliminate them altogether? What if it were possible to break up the cycles of poverty and community disinvestment? That's the journey we are on and we are not waiting for someone to develop the "app" to fix this, we are doing it ourselves. Together!

People from all walks of life, in organizations and

businesses all over this city are putting in the hard work to find new ways to work together, to plan together and create new ideas for revitalizing our neighborhoods.

Are there some things that we could do better? Yes, we have a long "to-do" list, to be sure. But we will not wait for "perfect", when so much "good" can come now. We will not miss the opportunity to invest our time, money, and resources in improving the systems that determine how our neighborhoods grow and function.

Today, we stand on the shoulders of decades of authentic community development from hundreds of people across this city, holding a steadfast commitment to racial justice, climate resilience, and shared prosperity. Through collaboration with local and national nonprofits, banks, corporate and civic leaders, we are shifting the model of how our city invests in people and our neighborhoods over the long-term.

Principle #9: Reimagine Your Value Proposition

Of all the principles of casemaking, this is often the one that is most counter-intuitive for the organizations I work with. Most organizations start their presentations off with a narrative about who they are and then go through a long-winded explanation of what they do, in the service of their communities. Then, they start credentialing the problems they work on and why those are the absolute WORST problems at the moment facing the community – which of course necessitates the need for their stakeholders to bring aid and resources to fix what's wrong. For most organizations, that stands in for their assessment of their value proposition.

That narration is not so much wrong as it is ill-suited if the goal is to get new champions for your work. Starting by talking all about who you are and what you do, can leave your audiences cheering for you but not feeling at all connected to your success nor fully understanding their role in your work.

So, we not only have to start the conversation differently (start with the aspirations of the people you are talking to, as Principle #1 suggests), then make your case (Principles #2 through 7) and

THEN...you get to talk about the unique value proposition of YOUR organization.

Yes, I'm suggesting that you turn your entire presentation upside down! For your audiences and stakeholders to WANT to work with you, they have to understand YOUR value proposition but that has to come much later in your materials, presentations or other casemaking that you do. Once you've made a strong case for the work, then your audiences will need to know more about why you are the best organization or coalition to lead or support that work in the unique way that you do. They'll need to understand what you are trying to do, how it matters or affects them, and that you have the credibility or a proven track record to get results.

Whether in business, sports or in social change efforts, people want to know that they are aligning themselves with "winners" and with people who can deliver on the promises they make. In a world where people are cynical about progress; where people hold little trust in leaders; where politicians promise the moon, stars, and planets to get our votes, but seldom deliver - the ability to deliver on those promises is what people value most.

So, our task is to help our stakeholders and strategic partners see the value in working with us and to trust our expertise, approach, theory of change, adaptive leadership AND our record of success. This means that we must articulate our track record, our uniqueness in some way, and the value-add that a collaboration would offer up.

This is our opportunity to share why our work, organization or coalition is best positioned to resolve the adaptive challenge or issue that we've identified in the case that we are making.

Be clear though - this does NOT mean offering up a list of your collective accomplishments in resume fashion, it means helping people see your value in the way that YOU see your value.

Sharing your value proposition starts with a strong theory of change or theory of action. When you are clear about the specific ways in which your organization or coalition will achieve the change it was created to serve (theory of change) and what actions it will take to get there (theory of action), you'll be much better at sharing that effectively with the stakeholders who you need to champion your efforts.

Often, the best way to share the theory of change is with a metaphor that describes why your work is different. More specifically, a metaphor that compares your approach to the status quo, helps your stakeholders see why your organization's approach and theory of change, is a big improvement over what already exists. The metaphor, in particular, should also do some heavy lifting in helping you underscore what your organization actually does – helping your potential champions better understand your work.

Here's an example of using a metaphor to share the value proposition – effectively distinguishing your approach from the status quo.

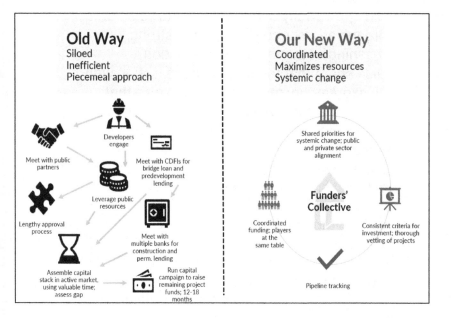

Reflection Questions

- Did I make my case first and THEN connect my audiences to the proven track record that my organization or my coalition has on this issue? (Note: If we do not yet have a track record, have we established trust and credibility on this issue with our stakeholders and strategic partners?)
- Did I powerfully communicate the value of my organization or coalition with a strong, meaningful theory of change/action?
- Did I share that theory of change/action with an explanatory metaphor to help give that theory real-time value to my stakeholders?
- Did I use that theory of change/action and metaphor to also help my audiences and stakeholders understand THEIR role in working with my organization and/or our coalition?

Your Ticket to Implementing This Principle

Typically, people focus on the wrong information when they try to position their value proposition and make a plug for their work at the wrong place in the narrative - starting their messaging with who they are and what they do. Yikes! Instead, push that information down in the narrative AFTER you've made a strong case on the issues you are trying to solve. Then, use a strong metaphor to help bring your theory of change/action, to life!

This is also a great place to bring in your impact data – data that shares what your impact has already been on this issue and to project with those data, what additional help/resources would do to advance your results even further. Don't assume here though "data" means only quantitative information, use qualitative data (stories, personal experiences, pictures, artistry, etc.) to distinguish your value proposition from the status quo.

Sample Success Measures

- ☐ **KPI:** We are consistently sharing our theory of change/action with our stakeholders after they have bought into the urgency and relevance of this issue.
- ☐ **Outcome:** Our stakeholders are operating with a clear understanding of our respective roles in resolving this issue.
- ☐ **Impact:** Our stakeholders are consistently working with us in ways that align with our theory of change/action.

HELPING YOUR STAKEHOLDERS AND STRATEGIC PARTNERS UNDERSTAND YOUR VALUE

Most of the time when people are offering advice about how to communicate a value proposition, they are talking about the solution you offer to your customers, clients or community. Positioning your organization and the contribution it can make however is much more about the value that you (or your coalition, agency, organization, company, collective impact group, etc.) brings to the table. It would be a big mistake to assume that people inherently understand why you are important to the process of finding or implementing solutions simply because you have formed a coalition, or collective impact group or neighborhood association, etc. Your stakeholders and strategic partners need to trust you and understand your role as well.

Unless people understand the systems you are trying to change and why you are best to lead that work, they won't fully commit to your call-to-action. So, take the time to position YOUR work and YOUR role carefully. In other words, help your stakeholders and strategic partners understand the value you bring.

As you work to do that, here are some pro-tips and guidelines to help you. There are five fundamental steps with plenty of room for embellishment.

Step 1: As a First Step, Show that You've Listened to What the Needs Are and Centered Those Voices Closest to the Problem You are Trying to Solve

- Always describe your first steps as LISTENING! (i.e., *As a first step to working in this community, we listened and learned from our community partners - residents, agencies, organizations, and companies*).

- Drill down into specific lessons taken from this deep listening that serves as a guide to your work. Highlight any particular lessons related to: (1) overcoming challenges to cross-sector alignment and collaboration, (2) nurturing leadership from all parts of the community, professional field or country as a whole; (3) translating lessons from the community or field into broader practice; (4) engaging community authentically and respectfully; and (5) creating a culture of wellness and resiliency across the board.

- Share how your listening helped to uncover nascent or emerging solutions on-the-ground or in practice. (*i.e., These efforts were under-powered because they were under-resourced and lacked the investments that could buy them the space and time to become stable anchors for resilience in their communities*).

- Share how the things you heard while in deep listening mode align (or differ from) existing practice or evidence. (*i.e., There has been important coalescence of the science on this issue that aligns with what we heard from community stakeholders*).

- Share the immediate next steps to be undertaken and why they require stakeholder alignment and new champions.

Step 2: Credential Your Leadership of the Effort.
- Share the track record (established history) of the team you've assembled.

  o Do they have experience leading or collaborating on similar efforts (especially those that are community-driven, equity-focused or multi-sector)?

- o Do they have experience addressing the specific issues on the table or are representing organizations that have this experience?

- Share how your effort builds on an important set of unique factors. It may be that the players around your table are unique or there is an unprecedented momentum emerging among stakeholders.

- Share what investments you and your collaborators have already made in addressing this issue and to what results.

- Share the ambitious vision that you have for solving that adaptive challenge collectively and why/how adding new strategic partners (i.e., new champions for this work) would help you gear up to do more.

- Share what core beliefs are driving this effort (*i.e., this effort exists because we believe there is great urgency and promise in providing support to community coalitions on the frontlines*).

Step 3: Share What Sets This Effort Apart from Past or Other Similar Efforts to Address This Issue.

- Share how the team assembled on this issue works together. Be specific. (*i.e. We do our work by identifying and testing new approaches in collaboration with other organizations, including both governmental agencies and private-sector entities*).
  - Are you working within a shared-equity model, advocacy, or collective impact model?
  - How does each member or organization provide consistent and appropriate leadership to the effort?

- Share how the work is funded and how you have worked to leverage funding for your effort.

- Share how your team uses evidence-based and community driven practices to drive its work.

- Share how your working relationships, programs, policies, services or investments have shifted over time (ostensibly because of your growing knowledge of what works).

- Share how you communicate your knowledge, best practices and other helpful supports back into the field or community in which you work.

- Share how this group is agile and nimble in its ability to respond to the dynamism that adaptive challenges often evoke.

Step 4: Be Clear About the Ways in Which You Partner with Other Mission Aligned Partners Who Do Similar Types of Work

When we share our value proposition with others, often the first question that comes back is – how are you different from x or y organization that is trying to solve the same (or a similar) problem? If you don't have an answer to that question, not only will you be caught flatfooted on the very thing that your value proposition and theory of change statements are meant to solve, but you may create unnecessary competition with other organizations doing equally important work.

So, the task is to get crystal clear – before you get in front of your stakeholders – how your work compliments but does not duplicate the important work that others are doing. As we say earlier in this chapter, one good way to distinguish your value proposition is to provide a metaphor that makes the distinctions clear.

Step 5: Be Prepared to Defer to Another Group of Leaders on Parts of the Work That You Do

Finally, be prepared to defer to another group of leaders in your coalition—if that seems like the right choice. It may be true that our organizations have been doing important work in a particular space for a long period of time. As our organizations evolve and as the context of our environments change, other organizations may have emerged with a more impactful solution, process, or approach.

If that happens, it doesn't automatically spell "lights out" for our approach, it just means that there may be an opportunity for us to swim further upstream – solving bigger or tangent issues that remain to be solved. Our strategic planning processes should help guide us on that path.

The task here is not to be afraid to relinquish some of the work to other organizations who may have a stronger value proposition. Be clear on our value proposition and to keep iterating on it to ensure we are solving the issues that are unique to what we bring to the community.

Building a Better Future, One Resilient Community at a Time

We believe the future of our planet will be shaped by how we invest our resources. The investments our cities make today, have a huge impact on the quality of our lives, our planet, and our opportunities for wellness in the short and long-term. Big infrastructure investments made in public transit systems, economic development and land development, to name just a few, are going to reshape the landscape of many cities across our nation.

For example, city governments are one of the biggest investors in smart city technology. In 2022 the investment made by cities in smart tech is expected to top $250 billion and grow to $350 billion by 2023. The critical decisions to invest and allocate these resources as well as the timing and scope of those investments, will ultimately determine who gets connected to opportunity and who is left out.

That's why we have organized a national network to support cities as they work to cultivate equitable and inclusive ways of deploying these needed resources. As a national network working to support and assist cities in making decisions that expand opportunity and equity for all, we know that our partnerships are what determine our success. Our network exists because of the commitment of leaders across this country who all believe that there is great urgency and promise in supporting the emergence of community-led, multi-sector networks to ensure that our cities make thoughtful decisions.

In this way, our network serves a unique role in influencing a "new normal" in how cities invest and advance the needs of their communities and residents. As a convener and a collective group of national thought leaders on the issues of community investment, public health, public policy, climate resilience, and the environment, we bring together expertise from philanthropy, business and local government to address cities' most urgent challenges.

Acting as a collective network, rather than as a single organization or government agency, we are able to respond more effectively to a wider range of adaptive challenges facing our cities. From COV-19, to affordable housing, to education, opioid addiction, infrastructure needs and disaster planning, our network makes it possible for cities to get the best advice, counsel and relevant partners to the table quickly. With this network structure, we can respond nimbly and directly to the urgency of the challenges our cities face.

We know that our cities (large and small, urban and rural) are ground-zero for a range of adaptive challenges that can only be solved through multi-sector efforts alongside the voices, involvement and lived experience of community residents. That's why our network was created and why our nation has a huge stake in its success.

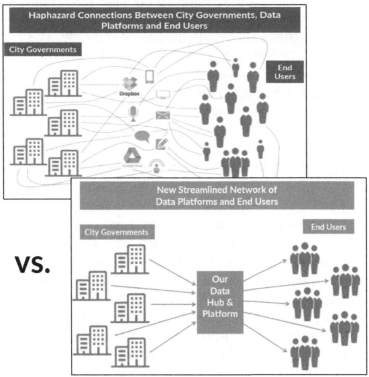

Principle #10: Share Your Roadmap and Metrics for Success

Like it or not, we live in a brand-new world of data. Data is collected everywhere and in every aspect of our lives. Many of us have become sophisticated in the collection of data about our issues and our stakeholders have come to expect that we have data to back up our claims that our approaches and solutions are working. The good news is that usually, the data is on our side. The impacts of the work that many of us are doing to improve our communities, cities and regions can be shown through an intentional focus on collecting the appropriate data.

Yet, in order to make a compelling case for more support, we need to wield this data carefully and strategically. Having a results framework with very specific data and metrics, makes it clear to stakeholders what the goal posts are and how they can trust that we're serious about driving toward the outcomes we laid out in our case. This means that we need to take seriously the charge of getting our numbers right. Understanding what the return-on-investment (ROI) is of our programs, policies and investments is critical – especially in today's world where so much of this information is easily calculated.

In addition, we need to ensure that we are also calculating the social-return-on-investment (SROI) or the impacts of our programs, policies and investments for our community. Seeing both the ROI and SROI next to each other, helps us provide empirical evidence.

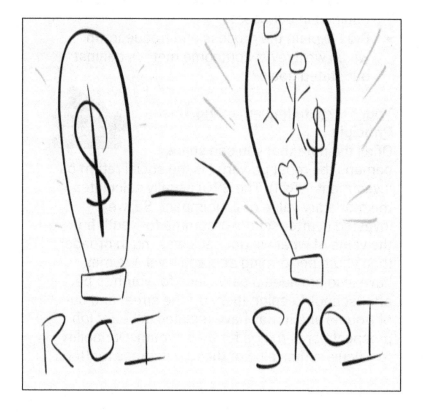

Reflection Questions

- Did I share the results framework (assessment of the short-term, mid-term & long-term outcomes as measures of success)?
- Am I calculating and sharing as part of my impact assessment, the ROI and SROI of my work?
- Did I share my theory of change/action to help my stakeholders understand what makes me confident that we will generate the outcomes outlined in our case?
- Did I explain the process and frequency in which we'll review outcome metrics against our stated goals?

Your Ticket to Implementing This Principle

Of all the data that you can share, perhaps the most powerful is the social return on investment (SROI). The SROI usually calculates the monetary value of your impact. So, we invested in after school programs for youth but the value of what we got back was much broader than youth performing at grade level. We may have also provided a safe place for youth to be after school, keeping them off the street and out of trouble and it may have resulted in better job prospects or earnings for those youth. Our ability to calculate the value of those outcomes matters!

Sample Success Measures

- [ ] **KPI:** We have defined a meaningful set of metrics, that we are consistently collecting and sharing broadly/transparently as part of our casemaking.
- [ ] **Outcome:** Our stakeholders have a clear understanding of what success means to us – in both qualitative and quantitative terms.
- [ ] **Impact:** Our stakeholders are more committed to our work because they understand that we are results focused and they help us to gather up the data we need to demonstrate progress on our issues.

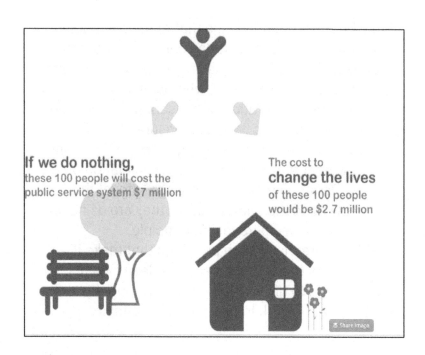

If we do nothing, these 100 people will cost the public service system $7 million

The cost to **change the lives** of these 100 people would be $2.7 million

INDUCING A "YES" STATE: SPOILER ALERT, METRICS MATTER!!!

There has always been a large body of scholarly research on the art or psychology of persuasion (some call it, the science of influence). In whatever variety it comes, the focus has always been – how do we get people to follow our lead and say "yes" to our call-to-action. For changemakers working to improve your communities, there is both an art and science involved in how you can make your case.

First, let's just acknowledge that many companies and individuals use methods—consciously or not—that behavioral science has shown are effective in getting people to say "yes", whether in making a sale, gaining cooperation or consensus, or coaxing charitable donations. When life insurance companies offer—with "no obligation"—a flashlight and keychain to AARP (American Association of Retired Persons) members who agree to let the company send them information, they are using an empirically-based persuasion principle.
And there are many such practices that make it easier for us to persuade people to lean in just long enough to give ourselves the opportunity to share how our work to bring about equitable

system change, might benefit all of us and the communities that surround us. Indeed, this book is a testament to that body of scholarship and evidence-based practice.

One of the most compelling techniques is the work you can do to induce a "yes" state. If you've ever been on a sales room floor for any appliance or to buy a car, you've been exposed to this principle. The car salesman might casually talk to you but ask a series of questions of you, as you browse the showroom floor. Some of those questions are meant to clarify if you are a serious buyer or just a "looky loo" perusing the salesroom floor as a spectator rather than a buyer. Once they've established that, they'll ask a series of questions meant to induce a "yes" state: the more often they can get you to say yes, even to small questions, the more likely they'll be able to get you to say yes to the big purchase.

So, the salesperson might start by saying something like, *"If I could get you the best financing rate on this car today, would you consider buying it today?"*

Once you've said yes, they'll proceed with more small talk and then say something like, *"and if I could get the make, model and color of your choice right here in the showroom today, would you consider buying it today?"*

Then, rinse, wash, and repeat...something like, *"And if I could get you a price that could beat anybody in this area, even under MSRP, then would you sit down with me and consider buying today?"* And so on...

The salesperson's purpose of those questions both qualifies you as a serious buyer and unbeknownst to you, induces a "yes" state. The salesperson is aiming at getting you to say "yes" at least seven times – why? The rule of seven in marketing is clear – the chances of the person saying "yes" to the big ask after seven yeses, increases dramatically. So, they want to throw you a pitch (or ask you softball "yes" questions) so that on the 7th throw, you are softened up and ready to go!

So, my friends, I'm not asking you to become a car salesman or peddle a marketing slide deck around with you. But I am asking you to be present to the idea that there are subtle ways of helping people connect with your call-to-action that are about human psychology. The more we understand those techniques, it allows us to be at least as persuasive as corporate marketers who peddle products to us (most of which we don't need and are over-priced).

So, get in the habit of preparing questions when you pitch your ideas that get people in the habit of saying yes. Something like:

- *"If I could show you how to improve health outcomes for the people in this community by at least 24% over the next year, with an investment the size of your paper towel budget, would you consider hearing me out?"*

- Or like this, *"If I could show you how to bring new resources to this community to improve the health and wellbeing of children in this community, with little to no personal investment, would you hear me out?"*

- Or, *"What if I could show you how to revitalize this community – bringing new playgrounds, open green space, bike zones, and more off-street parking, would you want to hear more about that?*

The questions you raise should be "no brainers". They should be easy "yes" questions that you know your stakeholders and strategic partners can say yes to.

Be mindful as well that the questions should accurately reflect what your call-to-action would actually do! Do NOT misrepresent what you can offer but give people a sense of what the benefits would be of leaning into your call-to-action.

To make this technique even more effective, make the "yes" question coincide with one or more of the success metrics you've laid out in your results framework. Like this,

- *"What if I could show we can bring down infant mortality rates in this community by 20% in 5 years, would you be interested?"*

- Or something like this, *"What if I told you that we have raised $13 million to support pilot programs and system innovations that are going to reduce homelessness in this community by more than 25% over the next 5 years, is that of interest to you?"*

- Or this one, *"Some people in this community are concerned about the number of children who have anxiety, depression or may be considering suicide. What if there are some simple ways that all of us can help cut that number in half in just under a year? It's been done in other communities, why not in ours?"*

People genuinely want to nod yes to those questions. Contrary to popular belief, they genuinely want to hear good news and when they hear more about the metrics of success that you've outlined for your work, you genuinely have a better shot at getting them to say "yes" to your call-to-action.

So, ASK QUESTIONS! Practice developing some good ones – ones that get people to think about the possibilities of your success and that help them understand your metrics for measurement. The opportunity to pull your audience forward using this technique is made even more effective when you pair it with your metrics of success.

When you use this pro-tip, you are able to pull people into a conversation saying "yes" before you get to the big ask and then, you can inspire them to share the good news of what your organization, agency or collaborative team is working on. It is also important to say again that metrics matter - no matter what – to our casemaking. They help convince our stakeholders and strategic partners that we are serious, that we have identified very specific outcomes and that we're willing to be held accountable for those outcomes.

Here's Our Results Framework. Track Our Progress, Help Us Celebrate the "Wins" and Improve in Areas Where We Are Struggling. We Need Your Help!

From the beginning of this effort, we have been relentlessly results-focused and accountability driven. We shared our results framework (the metrics we would use to ensure we were on target) early on in our process and we invite you now to help us evaluate how we're doing.

We've done quite a lot this year. So far, we've made significant and measureable progress in reducing our housing shortage and making homes a priority.

- ✓ We completed a strategic audit and action plan for our work this year.
- ✓ We developed and ratified Memoranda of Understanding (MOUs) among our collaborating organizations.
- ✓ We elevated leadership commitment on this issue with more than a dozen large employers in the region now championing this issue and committing resources.

- ✓ We have created stronger visibility on this issue so that media coverage, social media and local conferences all reflect a focus on this issue.
- ✓ We have strengthened the capacity of our advocacy partners by raising more than $25 million to support innovative programs for communities in the region.
- ✓ We have reduced point-in-time counts of people experiencing homelessness in our region through stronger lease-up rates.
- ✓ We have increased the ability of service providers to ramp up the operations, scale, and quality of services they offer.
- ✓ We have worked in strong cross-sector partnerships (with the consolidated school district, our teachers union and the largest hospitals across the region).

We are winning in the work to change the trajectory of this issue across our region. But there is stil much work to be done. We need public, nonprofit, and private sector leaders to join forces and meet this challenge head-on and with renewed vigor.

For the next three years of our partnership, we expect even bigger, measurable results that will shape our pathway to the broader impacts we are working toward. While some of the details around the next phase of our work will evolve over time, we believe it is important to chart out the pathway as we see it today. By 2028, we will:

- make homelessness rare, brief and non-recurring by accelerating our strategy and working with a wider range of partners
- eliminate chronic homelessness across our region
- have created an even stronger safety net for people who are housing insecure and vulnerable in the context of our housing system
- we will triple our capital raise on this issue – bringing in more than $150 million to support our strategies on this issue
- we will close the racial gap as it relates to homeownership and affordable rental housing, to ensure that people of color in our region are benefitting as much as other groups from our success
- we will strengthen the capacity of the community stakeholders and partners to scale the programs, services, and/organizational practices that deepen their impact by investing in new ideas and innovative solutions

- we will identify and build public support for a permanent revenue stream to ensure we are never again struggling to support the housing needs of so many people in our region

Join us to help transform our response to the housing needs of this region. Help us champion this effort in your network. You can help generate the groundswell of support we need to ensure the health of our region.

"We are unstoppable.

Another world is possible!"

Practice, Practice, Practice Starts Here

Like any other skills set, Strategic CaseMaking™ takes practice. Take this opportunity, having reviewed the principles to elevate your casemaking by using the pages that follow to practice. What would a strong opening statement look like that focused on your stakeholders' aspirations? What dominant narratives do you need to reframe to avoid the backfires that can reduce stakeholder support?

Take one or more of your externally-facing materials (your campaign materials, regional plan or strategic plan, your website language or mission statement) and use the examples in this book to practice. Think about how your stakeholders and strategic partners will receive what you're saying and what elements of your casemaking might best help to pull them forward.

START HERE!

Backfires, Backpack and Bedtime Stories

What are the Backfires we get as we try to make the case on this issue?

_____
_____
_____
_____
_____

- **What are the Backpacks we get as we try to make the case on this issue?**

_____
_____
_____
_____
_____
_____

- **What are the Bedtime Stories that people tell us when we try to make the case on this issue?**

_____
_____
_____
_____
_____
_____

Frame the Adaptive Challenge

The world is changing rapidly. How will our call-to-action on this issue prepare us for the world that is coming, the economy that is coming, the demographic & technological shifts that are coming, and for the planet we will inherit?

- Our adaptive challenge is:
  _____
  _____
  _____
  _____
  _____

- This adaptive challenge matters to all of us because:
  _____
  _____
  _____
  _____
  _____

- These are the resources, institutions, practices and skills sets we will need to solve this adaptive challenge:_____
  _____
  _____
  _____
  _____

Systems Change, Equity & Inclusion

To solve the adaptive challenge we face, we must be clear about the systems that need rethinking and how we can embody an inclusive process as we redesign those systems and achieve equitable outcomes as the result.

- **What systems would need to change for us to solve this adaptive challenge?**

  _____
  _____
  _____
  _____
  _____

- **What are the levers that drive change in those systems?**

  _____
  _____
  _____
  _____

- **What will equity and inclusion look like in the context of our call-to-action on systems change?**

  _____
  _____
  _____
  _____
  _____

The Bridge of Understanding

Let's be clear about who our champions are, as well as who could be new champions of our work, once we get them on the bridge of understanding.

- Who are the people, agencies, institutions, organizations, corporations, houses of worship, community residents, and others, who can influence change of those systems?

  _____
  _____
  _____
  _____

- What do we need from these potential champions? What's our theory of change about what happens once they are on the bridge of understanding:

  _____
  _____
  _____

- What are they afraid to lose? And, what are their dominant narratives about this issue?

  _____
  _____
  _____
  _____

Principles of Strategic CaseMaking™ Checklist

Principle 1: Have you tapped into the aspirations of the audiences you hope to inspire, move and call to action? Have you connected those aspirations to the work that you do? Have you made me the hero of your story?

Principle 2: Have you oriented me toward a future that inspires me? Have you helped me to see my agency in creating that future and have you made the current moment feel urgent for my action?

Principle 3: Have you made it clear what will be lost if I sit on the sidelines and don't lean into your work? (Loss for me personally as well as for my community and our nation).

Principle 4: Have you avoided triggering traps, like fear, fatalism, and zero sum thinking, that can halt or constrain progress? Have you countered the dominant narratives on the issues we work to address?

Principle 5: Are you focused on solutions rather than problems, especially with data? Do you have the data you need to support the solutions you offer? Do you describe solutions in ways that make them seem manageable, achievable and beneficial to everyone?

Principle 6: Do you lift up the need to fix antiquated and inequitable systems rather than people, individual corporations or specific groups of people?

Principle 7: Do you show an array of potential allies in the stories, pictures, and data you use to describe your work? Do you portray them as heroes in the stories you tell?

Principle 8: Do you make strong calls to collective responsibility and collective investment in the future we are building together? Do you lift up the need to share power with other community leaders to achieve mutual outcomes?

Principle 9: Do you portray yourselves as credible leaders with a strong track record of success?

Principle 10: Have you explained what success looks like and how you will measure and report on it?

Notes and Reflections

Notes and Reflections

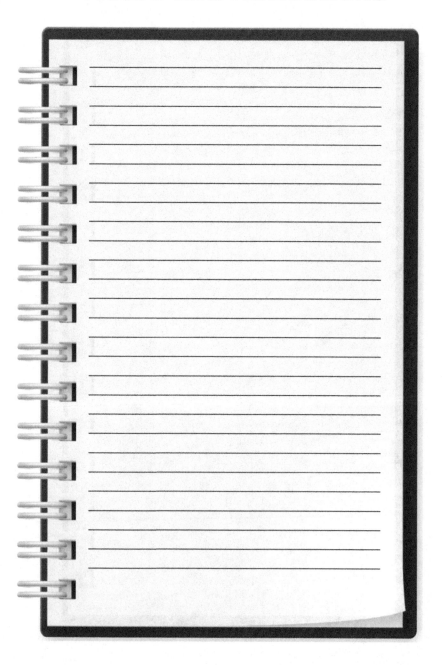

Notes and Reflections

Notes and Reflections

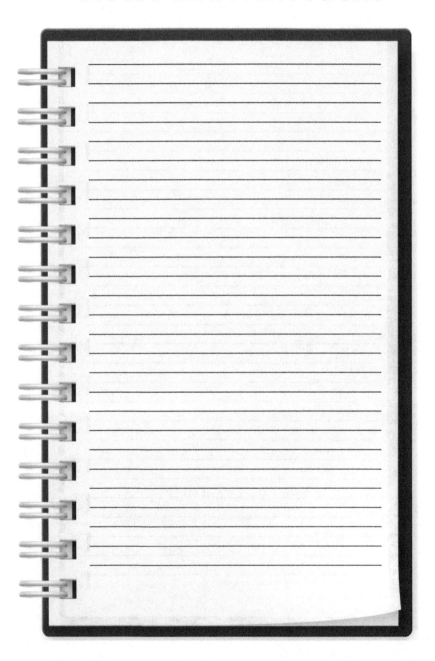

Notes and Reflections

Notes and Reflections

Notes and Reflections

Notes and Reflections

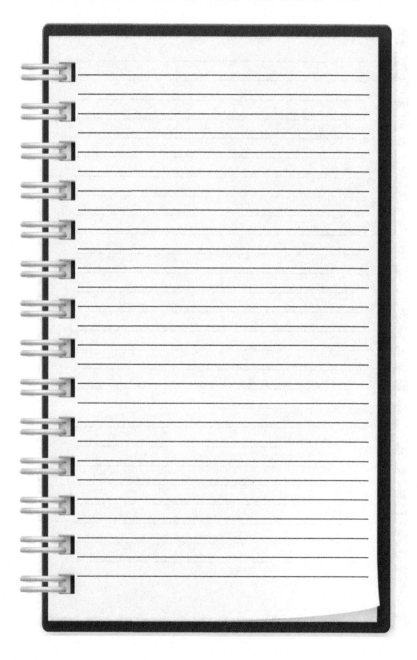

About **TheCaseMade**

Our mission is to transform communities all over the world by helping everyday heroes emerge as leaders. Those leaders reimagine how justice wins, by powerfully building the public will necessary to tackle the tough issues that determine our future.
We use trainings, workshops, community engagement and consulting to teach casemaking to leaders who can deliver strong impact.

At **TheCaseMade** we help leaders make the case for systems change by aligning stakeholders and organizing their resources in a deliberate system change strategy. We work across sectors and issue areas to help leaders understand the power of effective Strategic CaseMaking™ and to use it as a critical instrument for system change. Let us:

- facilitate a training or workshop to engage your staff, board, community partners and residents in Strategic CaseMaking™
- conduct a review of your public-facing materials to help provide recommendations for stronger casemaking
- support your executive team as strategic advisors in public-facing campaigns, strategic initiatives and cross-sector collaboration
- help refine your system change strategy by incorporating a meaningful way to measure success (an impact framework).

About the Author

Dr. Tiffany Manuel is the President and CEO of **TheCaseMade**, works with hundreds of passionate social change leaders, changemakers and innovators around the United States to help them powerfully and intentionally make the case for systems change.

Trained as a social scientist, DrT is committed to building the capacity of changemakers and leaders to grow their social impact. DrT has worked to expand opportunity for low-income workers, families and communities through 30+ years of professional and volunteer experience spanning the private and non-profit sectors, government and academia.

DrT is passionate about translating the insights harvested from this work to increase opportunities for public deliberation and public will-building. DrT holds doctorate and master's degrees in public policy from the University of Massachusetts Boston, a master's degree in political science from Purdue University and a bachelor's degree in political science from the University of Chicago.

Made in the USA
Coppell, TX
25 June 2024